Kanji Alchemy II
A Strategy for Reading Japanese Characters

Harry Nap

Copyright © 2015 Harry Nap

All rights reserved.

ISBN: -0-9941964-7-4
ISBN-13: - 978-0-9941964-7-7

CONTENTS

	Introduction	i
1	Aries	1
2	Taurus	28
3	Gemini	58
4	Cancer	84
5	Leo	111
6	Virgo	137
7	Libra	160
8	Scorpio	184
9	Sagittarius	207
10	Capricorn	230
11	Index & Definitions of Alchemical Symbols	253
12	Index Signature Characters	266
13	Bibliography & Online Resources	298

ACKNOWLEDGMENTS

Jim Breen's Kanjidic compilation of 6,355 kanji as specified in the JIS X0208 1990 standard has been used as the main source for Kanji Alchemy. This publication has included material from the JMdict (EDICT, etc.) dictionary files in accordance with the license provisions of the Electronic Dictionaries Research Group. See http://www.csse.monash.edu.au/~jwb/edict.html and http://www.edrdg.org/.

Kenneth Henshall's "A Guide to Remembering Japanese Characters" has been a major inspiration

INTRODUCTION

A different approach to kanji is required in order to facilitate reading proficiency:

- Start memorising kanji in groups or **clusters** rather than standalone characters.
- Study in a rational way by focusing on features within kanji that will aid kanji recognition such as **radicals** and an awareness of the etymology of the character.
- Study in a **systematic** way by imposing order and regularity on the multitude of characters. This means abandoning the conventional textbook format.

The second volume of Kanji Alchemy follows the same structure as the previous volume but with some changes. Whereas with General Use characters treated in Kanji Alchemy I the emphasis was on compound kanji, i.e. emphasising the fact that in texts kanji appear more frequently as words (combinations of more than one kanji) rather than as individual characters, this is with Jinmeiyou kanji no longer the case. Given the nature and frequency of these particular characters, often referring to flora & fauna, providing compound characters would seem less useful. This applies even more so to the set of Non General Use characters (Hyougaiji) in Kanji Alchemy III. Consequently (recall) sentences are no longer a feature in in the last two volumes as there is no reference to compound characters. Jinmeiyou kanji refer to a list of 862 characters that is maintained by the Ministry of Justice. Although sometimes added to the 2136 Joyou kanji -General Use characters- these are a distinct set of characters and should be treated separately.

人名用漢字 literally means "Chinese characters for use in personal names" and are used as registered personal, family and place names. The list has been revised a number of times with the last change occurring in 2015. There are 212 traditional forms or variants of Joyou kanji in the Jinmeiyou list. The remainder are 650 kanji (including variants) that do not appear in the set of Joyou kanji. Japanese characters have a structure that allows for a modicum of understanding. There are recurring features that provide clues and it is clear that there is some kind of consistency in the proliferation of different forms. Characters have their own story to tell and that message can be reinforced when they are grouped together and treated as a set or a cluster. Within each cluster, it is possible to designate one character as a point of reference. 490 of these characters have been selected to act as a chunking device, representing anything from 2 to 14 similar characters in the set. This new allocation of kanji represents a radical departure from the way in which Japanese characters have been studied until now. To focus on approximately 23% of selected General Use characters means a considerable reduction in memorization and learning. The same set of 490 signature characters has also be used in the "Jinmei" series of the second volume and in the "Non General Use" (NGU) characters of the third volume of Kanji Alchemy. The entire range of kanji amounts to 6460 characters. Following is a synopsis of the method.

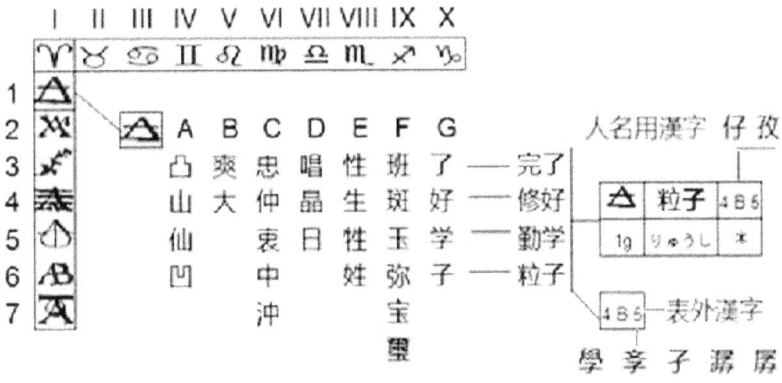

Note that there are ten chapters and that each chapter (named after a star sign) consists of seven weeks. Each week is represented by an alchemical symbol -the first week being AIR- containing seven days (A-G). The example of G shows that there are four characters in the General Use (Jouyou) Kanji range. The symbol in the left corner of the box features the glyph for AIR followed by the "Sight Word" and completed by information showing similar characters in Jinmei Kanji (A = 1, B = 2 etc.) and Non General Use Kanji (5).
Learning to read 2136 characters and compounds is a formidable

burden on the memory but it is a possible to considerably lessen this strain. Rather than exclusively focusing on memorization and retention, kanji recognition with an analytical focus should become one of the tools for coming to terms with Japanese characters. A case in point are the "semantic-phonetic" characters that represent 85% of all kanji. This category consists of two components: the phonetic component refers to the (long obsolete) pronunciation of the character (on-reading) while the semantic element indicates the meaning or context. An approach that highlights the salient features of kanji will significantly reduce reliance on memorization. A clear understanding of radicals, in particular the ones that function as a semantic or phonetic indicator in the constituent character, will make the learning process much more efficient. Each kanji has one defining radical that is designated as a dictionary index. Although there are 214 radicals, the most frequent 18 account for 50% usage and the most frequent 48 radicals cover 75%. Learning kanji means learning vocabulary in a convoluted way. Japanese vocabulary can broadly be classified into kango (words from Chinese origin or created from Chinese words), wago (native Japanese words) and garaigo (loanwords). Approximately 70% of dictionary entries are kanji compounds, the majority of these are kango. Kango consists of two (or more) kanji, each character having a reading that approximated the original Chinese at one stage (on-reading). Good knowledge of kango is indispensable for understanding texts. When learning how to read Japanese characters, strong emphasis should therefore be placed on kanji compounds. The key to more efficient study of kanji lies in the reordering of the 2136 general use characters. This is to be achieved through clustering and chunking. Clustering refers to the partitioning of a data set into subsets (clusters), so that the data in all subsets (ideally) share some common trait. Chunking is the practice of grouping units of information into smaller units or chunks in order to facilitate memorization. (signature characters) Just as a string of digits can be regrouped into a smaller number of meaningful units to form a date, Japanese characters can be re-arranged in order to emphasize shared elements that greatly facilitate recognition. Through careful selection 490 signature characters and their clusters represent over 1990 General Use Kanji. Each of these signature characters represents on average 3 to 4 other characters that share the same features; this means that over 90% of the General Use Kanji are related in a meaningful, learner-friendly way. Grouping together characters that share the same elements greatly facilitates the learning process and makes memorization less burdensome. In many cases radicals will make the distinction between characters that have common features. There are about 150 other characters in the 2136 General Use Kanji that are not related and are therefore not directly referenced to the signature characters. (7%) These characters feature of course in kanji compounds but seem to be otherwise singular, unique kanji such as some of the kanji denoting numerals (八 eight 百 hundred) as well as a number of pictographs (月 moon 毛 hair). This aspect changes when Jinmei and NGU kanji are considered: suddenly a great many of these characters become productive and in fact do have their own clusters of kanji with a similar structure. A "productive" non-related character is indicated by an asterisk. The vertical bar or pipe character (|) in the key will sometimes show double or triple vertical bars if more than one of the approximately 150 non related characters have similar forms. Consider 礼 courtesy, salute:

礼	禮	乢	紀	軋
Non Related	Jinmei (Old Form)	Non General Use	Non General Use	Non General Use

The same set of 490 signature kanji is also used for "Jinmei Kanji" (862 kanji that are allocated for writing names) and Non General Use Kanji (more than 3460 kanji that belong neither to the General Use nor the Jinmei category). Sight words and recall sentences form an integral part of the learning process. The sight word is a kanji compound (粒子 particle) that refers to a range of similar characters that are grouped (clustered) together and that acts as a chunking device. Rather than learning one character at a time, a cluster of kanji should be memorized as a group and associated with the relevant signature character in a sight word. Sight words are sometimes used in English reading classes to teach young children high frequency words that are difficult to explain with phonics. (There are various, strongly disagreeing points of view on this subject.) It is part of the whole-word approach that emphasizes visual recognition of a word without analysis of the sub-parts after which the child is able to pronounce the whole word as a single unit. Given the large variety of kanji readings in the Japanese context, a visual approach makes sense because phonological clues are generally not so helpful. The relevant character that is used in the sight word is a bare or "stripped down" version of the similar kanji it represents, i.e. a character with the least complex radical of the kanji in the cluster or containing no radical at all. When the appropriate radicals are added to the character, the other related kanji in the group will become apparent. This applies not only to the 2136 general use characters but also, often to an even larger extent, to Jinmei and Non General Use characters as well.

A **recall sentence** is a verbal representation of all the characters in the cluster. In the 1G example this would be: **Completed a fine study in small parts**. (Completion 完了, friendship 修好, studying while working 勤学 and particle 粒子) The sentence functions as a mnemonic device incorporating all the compounds of the specific kanji. The recall sentence refers to the other General Use Kanji with a similar structure in the order in which they have been learned making retrieval of relevant information much easier.

The learning process involves the expansion from one character to many: **signature character**; 子 **sight word**; 粒子 **sentence**; 完了/修好/勤学/粒子 **story**; "Notes from the House of Fashion", a short story for practicing kanji that covers a number of the characters featuring in that particular week. (See first week Kanji Alchemy I). It should be noted that, as kanji clusters cover the entire range of General Use Kanji, the conventional order of starting with only "Education Kanji" is no longer the case. Common elements in the structure of kanji can occur anywhere. This means that along with frequent characters – Education Kanji, the first 1006-- less frequent characters in the General Use Kanji range are introduced from the beginning of the series. The use of transliterated Japanese (romaji) should be discouraged. The convention of having katakana for on-reading and hiragana for kun-reading is to be followed. It is less effective to use romaji as it adds an extra step to the learning process. To use kana prepares for future use of Japanese-only materials and maps kanji to pronunciation in the most direct way.

A more elaborate overview of kanji and Kanji Alchemy can be found on www.kanjialchemy.com

CHAPTER 1 ARIES

1A 山 AIR

△	仙術	4A7
1A 並	せんじゅつ	*

Pictograph of a mountain 山
Representation of convexity 凸

山	サン、やま	mountain	1A
辿	テン、たど-る	follow (road); pursue	辿

1B 大 AIR

△	大寒	2A1
1B	だいかん	*

Pictograph of a standing person 大

大	ダイ、タイ、おお、おお-きい、おお-いに	big	1B
尖	セン、とが-る	be pointed	尖

1C 実 AIR

△	中立	5–3
1C	ちゅうりつ	1‖2

Originally string of money under a roof, wealthy, substantial 実

実	ジツ、み、みの-る	(bear) fruit, truth, reality	1C
實	VARIANT OF 実	(bear) fruit, truth, reality	實

1D 日 AIR

△	翌日	3B8
1D	よくじつ	*

Pictograph of the sun 日

日	ニチ、ジツ、ひ、か	sun, day	1D
菖	ショウ	iris	菖
昌	ショウ、さか-ん	prosperous; bright; clear	昌

1E 生 AIR

△	性分	4A2

| 1E | しょうぶん | 0‖5 |

Growing plant 生

| 生 | セイ、ショウ、い-きる、い-かす、い-ける、う-まれる、う-む、お-う、は-える、は-やす、き-なま | life, birth, grow | 1E |
| 笙 | ショウ | a reed instrument | 笙 |

1F 玉 AIR

| ⌒ | 目玉 | 6D8 |
| 1F | めだま | * |

Originally string of beads, jade 玉
Originally device used in spinning, phonetic to press into clay/earth 璽

璽	ジ	imperial seal	1F
爾	ジ、なんじ、のみ	you	爾
禰	ネ、デイ、ナイ	ancestral shrine	禰
祢	ALTERNATIVE OF 禰	ancestral shrine	祢

| 弥 | ミ、ビ、いやや、あまねし、いよいよ | all the more; increasingly | 1F |
| 彌 | VARIANT OF 弥 | all the more; increasingly | 彌 |

1G 子 AIR

| ⌂ | 粒子 | 4B5 |
| 1G | りゅうし | * |

Infant wrapped in clothes 子

子	シ、ス、こ	child	1G
仔	シ	offspring	仔
孜	シ、つと-める	industriousness	孜

2A 化 ALEMBIC

| ⋈ | 化け物 | 3A6 |
| 2A | ばけもの | 6‖12 |

Standing person, fallen person, change 化
Cow and variety of streamers, creature, thing 物

Possibly variant of watch tower, high, raised earth 壇

花	カ、はな	flower, blossom	2A
椛	かば、もみじ	birch; maple	椛
物	ブツ、モツ、もの	thing	2A
忽	コツ、たちま-ち	in a moment; instantly; all of a sudden; neglect; disregard	忽
惚	コツ、ぼ-ける、ほ-れる	fall in love with; admire; grow senile	惚
惣	ソウ	all	惣
勿	ブツ、モチ、な-かれ	not; must not; do not; be not	勿
吻	フン、くちびる	proboscis	吻
壇	ダン、タン	stage, rostrum, podium	2A
檀	ダン、まゆみ	cedar; sandalwood; spindle tree	檀

2B 丁 ALEMBIC

| ⚚ | 丁寧 | 7D9 |
| 2B | ていねい | 0\|5 |

Originally nail (now ngu character + metal) 丁

丁	チョウ、テイ	block, exact	2B
庁	チョウ	government, office, agency	2B
廳	VARIANT OF 庁	government, office, agency	廳
灯	トウ、ひ	light, lamp	2B
燈	VARIANT OF 灯	light, lamp	燈
釘	テイ、くぎ	nail; tack; peg	釘
汀	テイ、なぎさ、みぎわ	water's edge; shore; bank	汀

2C 車 ALEMBIC

⚗	車庫	5D6
2C	しゃこ	*

Two-wheeled chariot 車

転	テン、ころ-がる、ころ-げる、ころ-がす、ころ-ぶ	rotate, roll, tumble	2C
轉	VARIANT OF 転	rotate, roll, tumble	轉
轟	ゴウ、とどろ-く	roar; thunder; boom, resound	轟
蓮	レン、はす	lotus	蓮

| 漣 | レン、さざなみ | ripples | 漣 |

2D 立 ALEMBIC

| ⚗ | 立場 | 5A4 |
| 2D | たちば | * |

Originally person standing on the ground 立

| 立 | リツ、リュウ、た-つ、た-てる | stand, rise, leave | 2D |
| 笠 | リュウ、かさ | bamboo hat; one's influence | 笠 |

2E 石 ALEMBIC

| ⚗ | 嫉妬 | 4C4 |
| 2E | しっと | * |

Cliff and (carved out) rock/boulder 石

石	セキ、シャク、コク、いし	stone, rock	2E
柘	シャ、つげ	wild mulberry	柘
宕	トウ	cave	宕

| 碧 | ヘキ、あお、みどり | blue | 碧 |

2F 字 ALEMBIC

⚛	字幕	2–3
2F	じまく	*

Originally house where children are raised, proliferation, numerous letters 字

2G 目 ALEMBIC

⚛	目撃者	4–5
2G	もくげきしゃ	*

Pictograph of an eye 目

3A 先 ALUM

	指先	2A2
3A	ゆびさき	1|3

Originally foot/stop + person, die, ancestors, precede, tip 先
Originally kneeling at the altar 礼

| 先 | セン、さき | previous, precede, tip | 3A |

銑	セン	pig iron	銑
礼	レイ、ライ	courtesy, salute, bow	3A
禮	VARIANT OF 礼	courtesy, salute, bow	禮

3B 左 ALUM

✄	左側	3B7
3B	ひだりがわ	*

Left hand + work upon, auxiliary, assist 左

左	サ、ひだり	left	3B
嵯	サ	steep; craggy; rugged	嵯
瑳	サ、みが-く	polish	瑳

3C 十 ALUM

✄	十字路	4A4
3C	じゅうじろ	*

Sewing needle used as a substitute for more a complex character 十

十	ジュウ、ジッ、とお、と	ten	3C
辻	つじ	crossing; crossroad; street corners	辻

3D 足 ALUM

✻		満足	4A1
3D		まんぞく	0|4

Foot and kneecap, lower leg, able 足

踏	トウ、ふ-む、ふ-まえる	tread, step on	3D
沓	トウ、くつ	shoes	沓

3E 青 ALUM

✻		青春	7C7
3E		せいしゅん	1||10

Growth around a full well, fresh, green, immature 青
Originally showing exuberant growth of a mulberry plant + sun 春

青	セイ、ショウ、あお、あお-い	blue, green, young	3E
静	セイ、ジョウ、しず、しず-か、しず-まる、しず-める	quiet, calm	3E
靜	VARIANT OF 静	quiet, calm	靜
錆	セイ、さび	tarnish	錆
靖	セイ、やす-い	peaceful	靖
春	シュン、はる	spring	3E
椿	チン、つばき	camellia	椿

3F 魚 ALUM

✶		魚貝	2–6
3F		ぎょかい	3|2

Originally pictograph of a pointed bivalve 貝
Pictograph of a fish 魚

魚	ギョ、うお、さかな	fish	3F
蘇	ソ、よみが-える	be resuscitated; revived	蘇
魯	ロ、おろ-か	foolish; Russia	魯

櫓	ロ、やぐら	oar; tower	櫓

3G 万 ALUM

✦	発音	7–5
3G	はつおん	1|2

Originally form of speak with addition of tongue 音
Older form is a pictograph of a scorpion 万

万	マン、バン	ten thousand	3G
萬	VARIANT OF 万	ten thousand	萬

4A 七 AMALGAM

秊	七面倒	3–2
4A	しちめんどう	0|2

Vaguely resembling a bent finger under a fist, old way to indicate seven 七

4B 空 AMALGAM

盃	寒空	2A4
4B	さむぞら	*

Hole (open space under roof) + work upon 空

空	クウ、そら、あ-く、あ-ける、から	sky, empty	4B
腔	コウ	body cavity	腔

4C 耳 AMALGAM

盃	取出す	5H21
4C	とりだす	0|3

Pictograph of a pointed ear 耳

耳	ジ、みみ	ear	4C
摂	セツ、ショウ、おさ.める、かね.る、と.る	surrogate; act in addition to	4C
攝	VARIANT OF 摂	surrogate; act in addition to	攝
諏	シュ	consult	諏

輯	シュウ、あつ-める	gather; collect; compile	輯
葺	シュウ、ふ-く	thatch; cover; shingle; tile	葺
茸	ジョウ、きのこ、たけ	mushroom	茸
叢	ソウ、くさむら	plexus; clump of bushes; thicket	叢
耶	ヤ、か、や	question mark	耶
椰	ヤ、やし	coconut tree	椰

4D 見 AMALGAM

衾	見易い	4C4
4D	みやすい	*

Eye and (formerly) bent legs, kneeling to stare at something 見

見	ケン、み-る、み-える、み-せる	look, see, show	4D
寛	カン	magnanimous, relax	4D
寛	VARIANT OF 寛	magnanimous, relax	寛
視	シ	see, look, regard	4D

視	VARIANT OF 視	see, look, regard	視
硯	ケン、すずり	ink stone	硯

4E 九 AMALGAM

杰	九折	4B4
4E	きゅうせつ	*

Bent elbow = nine when counting with one arm 九

九	キュウ、ク、ここの、ここの-つ	nine	4E
鳩	キュウ、あつ-める、はと	pigeon; dove	鳩
旭	キョク、あさひ	rising sun; morning sun	旭

4F 交 AMALGAM

杰	外交	6–13
4F	がいこう	*

Pictograph of person sitting with crossed legs, mix 交

4G 夕 AMALGAM

夜	夕空	4A2
4G	ゆうぞら	*

Pictograph of a crescent moon 夕

夕	セキ、ゆう	evening		4G
汐	セキ、うしお、しお	eventide; tide; saltwater; opportunity		汐

5A 六 ANTIMONY

⚘	六角	2-7
5A	ろっかく	*

Originally roof, then used as a substitute for clenched fist; six 六

5B 正 ANTIMONY

⚘	正直	8B8
5B	しょうじき な	0|1

Originally variant of lower leg, straight, proper/correct 正

正	セイ、ショウ、ただ-しい、ただ-す、まさ	correct	5B
淀	デン、よど	pool; eddy	淀
柾	まさ	straight grain; spindle tree	柾

5C 分 ANTIMONY

⚛	分子	6–9
5C	ぶんし	0‖3

Split, sword/cut 分

5D 赤 ANTIMONY

⚛	赤面	3–3
5D	せきめん	*

Originally big fire with ruddy glow 赤

5E 来 ANTIMONY

⚛	姉妹	4–1
5E	しまい	3|10

Tree with additional branches at the top, still growing 未
Pictograph of a wheat plant 来

来	ライ、く-る、きた-る、きた-す	come	5E
來	VARIANT OF 来	come	來
萊	ライ、あかざ	goosefoot; pigweed	萊
徠	ライ、く-る	induce; encourage to come	徠

5F 今 ANTIMONY

⊕	吟詠	7B9
5F	ぎんえい	1|3

Cover, put in a corner conceal 今
Pictograph of a tendon 力

今	コン、キン、いま	now	5F
衿	キン、えり	neck; collar; lapel	衿
稔	ネン、みの-る	harvest; ripen	稔
力	リョク、リキ、ちから	strength, effort	5F
肋	ロク、あばら	rib	肋

5G 虫 ANTIMONY

♁	蛍雪	6–9
5G	けいせつ	0|4

Insect 虫

6A 土 ARMENIAN BOLE

♃	土煙	3D3
6A	つちけむり	0|4

Pictograph of a clod of earth on the ground 土

土	ド、ト、つち	earth	6A
社	シャ、やしろ	company, Shinto shrine	6A
社	VARIANT OF 社	company, Shinto shrine	社
庄	ショウ	level	庄
杜	ト、もり	woods; grove	杜
牡	ボ、お、おす	-male	牡

6B 王 ARMENIAN BOLE

AB	王位	4D16
6B	おうい	*

Originally blade of a large battle axe 王
Originally expressing king and crown 皇

王	オウ	king; rule; magnate	6B
匡	キョウ、すく-う、ただ-す	correct	匡
皇	コウ、オウ	emperor	6B
凰	オウ、おおとり	female phoenix bird	凰
煌	コウ、かがや-く、きら-めく	glitter	煌
鳳	ホウ、おおとり	male mythical bird	鳳

6C 園 ARMENIAN BOLE

AB	公園	3B7
6C	こうえん	1|4

Chinese only long robe, phonetic long 園
Pictograph of swirling within an enclosure 回

園	エン、その	garden, park	6C
薗	ALTERNATIVE OF 園	garden, ark	薗
蓑	サ、みの	straw raincoat	蓑
回	カイ、エ、まわ-る、まわ-す	turn, rotate	6C
廻	エ、カイ、まわ-る、めぐ-る	round; game; revolve; go around; circumference	廻

6D 白 ARMENIAN BOLE

| AB | 告白 | 6C5 |
| 6D | こくはく | * |

Literally thumbnail, white 白

伯	ハク	count, senior figure	6D
箔	ハク	foil; gilt	箔
珀	ハク	amber	珀
柏	ハク、かしわ	oak	柏

6E 色 ARMENIAN BOLE

⁂	好色	4E7
6E	こうしょく	*

Person bending over another person 色

肥	ヒ、こ-える、こえ、こ-やす、こ-やし	fatten, enrich	6E
杷	ハ	kind of rake	杷
琶	ハ	lute	琶
芭	バ	banana	芭
巴	ハ、ともえ	comma-design	巴
邑	ユウ、むら	village; rural community; right village radical	邑

6F 同 ARMENIAN BOLE

⁂	銅像	5A2
6F	どうぞう	*

Possible variant of boat, convey + mouth/say (the same thing?) 同

| 同 | ドウ、おな-じ | same | 6F |
| 桐 | トウ、きり | paulownia | 桐 |

6G 系 ARMENIAN BOLE

| ᴁ | 系統 | 7A3 |
| 6G | けいとう | 0\|7 |

Pictogram of skein of yarn, originally doubled 系

| 系 | ケイ | lineage, connection | 6G |
| 胤 | イン、たね | descendent | 胤 |

7A 田 ATHANOR

| 困 | 田打ち | 4B12 |
| 7A | たうち | * |

Pictograph of a rice field 田

| 田 | デン、た | rice field | 7A |

| 佃 | デン、つくだ | cultivated rice field | 佃 |
| 畠 | はた、はたけ | field; farm; garden | 畠 |

7B 工 ATHANOR

| 𝔸 | 大工 | 8A8 |
| 7B | だいく | * |

Carpenter's adze-cum-square 工

| 工 | コウ、ク | work | 7B |
| 鴻 | コウ、おおとり | large bird; wild goose | 鴻 |

7C 明 ATHANOR

| 𝔸 | 克明 | 2B |
| 7C | こくめい | 0\|2 |

Sun and moon symbolising light, very bright 明

| 明 | メイ、ミョウ、あ-かり、あか-るい、あか-るむ、あか-らむ、あき-らか、あ-ける、あ-く、あ-くる、あ-かす | clear, open, bright | 7C |

萌	ホウ、きざ-す、めぐ-む、も-える	show symptoms of; sprout; bud; malt	萌
萠	VARIANT OF 萌	show symptoms of; sprout; bud; malt	萠

7D 寸 ATHANOR

🅐	一寸	10A8
7D	いっすん	1|9

Originally pulse being one sun (width of finger) from base palm 寸
Originally expressing a hunting dog leaping on a prey 猟

寸	スン	measure, inch	7D
団	ダン、トン	group, body, mass, ball, round	7D
團	VARIANT OF 団	group, body, mass, ball, round	團
猟	リョウ	game-hunting; shooting; game; bag	7D
蠟	ロウ、みつろう、ろうそく	wax	蠟

7E 己 ATHANOR

𝔸	自己	7B3
7E	じこ	*

Twisted thread, first person pronoun 己

己	コ、キ、おのれ	I, me, you, self	7E
已	イ、のみ、や-む	stop	已
巳	シ、み	sign of the snake or serpent	巳

7F 合 ATHANOR

𝔸	合唱	6B14
7F	がっしょう	*

Lid, cover, mouth say, cap off remark, reply fittingly 合

合	ゴウ、ガッ、カッ、あ-う、あ-わす、あ-わせる	meet, join, fit	7F
閤	コウ	small side gate	閤
恰	コウ、あたか-も	just as; as though; fortunately	恰

7G 北 ATHANOR

A	敗北	2A5
7G	はいぼく	*

Originally two persons sitting back to back, coldest direction 北

北	ホク、きた	north, flee	7G
燕	エン、つばめ	swallow (bird)	燕

CHAPTER 2 TAURUS

8A 内 BALM

♉	獄内	2–6
8A	ごくない	0|1

Originally enter + dwelling = inside 内

8B 広 BALM

♉	広告	3B9
8B	こうこく	*

Originally spacious building illuminated by flaming arrow 広

広	コウ、ひろ-い、ひろ-まる、ひろ-める、ひろ-がる、ひろ-げる	wide, spacious	8B
廣	VARIANT OF 広	wide, spacious	廣
弘	グ、コウ、ひろ-い	vast; broad; wide	弘

8C 馬 BALM

馬	馬乗り	6A10
8C	うまのり	*

Pictograph of a horse 馬

| 騒 | ソウ、さわ-ぐ | noise, disturbance | 8C |
| 騒 | VARIANT OF 騒 | noise, disturbance | 騒 |

8D 陽 BALM

陽	太陽	8C11
8D	たいよう	0|4

Chinese only bright and open out, sun rising high and shining down 陽

Originally expressing misty/shady side of the hill 陰

湯	トウ、ゆ	hot water	8D
暢	チョウ、の-ばす	stretch	暢
楊	ヨウ、やなぎ	willow	楊
陰	イン、かげ、かげ-	shadow, secret, negative (yin)	8D

	る		
蔭	イン、かげ	shade; shadow; backing assistance	蔭

8E 首 BALM

ꙮ	首肯	4A2
8E	しゅこう	*

Originally eye with exaggerated eyebrow, eye area of face 首 Countenance and phonetic 貌

首	シュ、くび	head, neck, chief	8E
貌	ボウ、かお、かたち	appearance	8E
兜	トウ、かぶと	helmet; head piece	兜

8F 売 BALM

ꙮ	売り物	4A9
8F	うりもの	*

Formerly to buy, put out for buying; sell 売

売	バイ、う-る、う-れる	sell	8F
賣	VARIANT OF 売	sell	賣

8G 池 BALM

池	用水池	3C3
8G	ようすいち	0|1

Twisting creature, snake undulating ground 池

池	チ、いけ	pond, lake	8G
弛	シ、たゆ-む、ゆる-む	slacken; relax	弛
馳	チ、は-せる	run; gallop; sail; drive (a wagon); win (fame); despatch	馳
也	ヤ、なり、また、や	to be (classical)	也

9A 楼 BATH OF VAPOURS

𝖁𝖁	鐘楼	3A22

9A	しょうろう	*

Shamaness chanting whilst holding counting stick 楼

桜	オウ、さくら	cherry	9A
櫻	VARIANT OF 桜	cherry	櫻

9B 里 BATH OF VAPOURS

9B	古里	5E13
9B	ふるさと	2|3

Ground with fields and dividing paths, settlement 里
Originally dancing person, borrowed phonetic to express "not" 無

里	リ、さと	village, league	9B
纏	テン、まと-う	wear	纏
裡	リ、うち	reverse; inside; palm; sole; rear; lining; wrong side	裡
鯉	リ、こい	carp	鯉
浬	リ、ノット	knot; nautical mile	浬
哩	リ、マイル	mile	哩

無	ム、ブ、な-い	non, non, cease to be		9B
蕪	ブ、あ-れる、かぶ	turnip		蕪
撫	ブ、な-でる	stroke; pat; smooth down		撫

9C 黄 BATH OF VAPOURS

ᚼB		黄色		3C
9C		きいろ		*

Original meaning flaming arrow, yellow 黄

黄	コウ、オウ、き、こ	yellow	9C
黄	VARIANT OF 黄	yellow	黄
横	オウ、よこ	side, crossways	9C
横	VARIANT OF 横	side, crossways	横
寅	イン、とら	sign of the tiger	寅

9D 家 BATH OF VAPOURS

ᚼB		作家		3A7

9D	さっか	*

Pictograph of a pig 家

家	カ、ケ、いえ、や	house, specialist	9D
蒙	モウ、くら-い、こうむ-る	ignorance; darkness; get; receive; be subjected to; sustain; Mongolia	蒙

9E 原 BATH OF VAPOURS

⑤	原子	4–1
9E	げんし	*

Cliff + variant of spring 原

9F 斗 BATH OF VAPOURS

⑤	北斗星	3–6
9F	ほくとせい	*

Pictograph of a ladle 斗

9G 戸 BATH OF VAPOURS

⑤	戸籍	5B5

| 9G | こせき | * |

Pictograph of "half" a door 戸

戸	コ、と	door	9G
肇	チョウ、はじ-め	beginning	肇
芦	ロ、あし、よし	reed, bulrush	芦

10A 申 BISMUTH

ℬ	申し込む	6E16
10A	もうしこむ	*

Originally forked lightning, 'voice of the gods?' 申

申	シン、もう-す	say, expound	10A
神	シン、ジン、かみ、かん、こう	god, spirit	10A
神	VARIANT OF 神	god, spirit	神
庵	アン、いお、いおり	hermitage	庵
曳	エイ、ひ-く	pull	曳
奄	エン、たちま-ち	cover	奄

榊	さかき		sacred Shinto tree	榊

10B 作 BISMUTH

ℬ		製作	5A9
10B		せいさく	*

Non General Use character adze on wood, make/construct 作

作	サク、サ、つく-る	make		10B
窄	サク、すぼ-む、せま-い	narrow; fold; furl; shrug; pucker; shut; close		窄

10C 弱 BISMUTH

ℬ		文弱	2B6
10C		ぶんじゃく	*

Doubling of bow, bending and delicate hairs, easily bent 弱

弱	ジャク、よわ-い、よわ-る、よわ-まる、よわ-める		weak	10C

鰯	いわし		sardine	鰯
粥	シュク、かゆ		rice gruel	粥

10D 曜 BISMUTH

B		曜日	3D3
10D		ようび	*

Bird and wings, passing 曜

曜	ヨウ	day of the week	10D
擢	テキ、ぬ-きんでる	excel in; surpass; pull out; select	擢
櫂	トウ、かい	oar; scull; paddle	櫂
耀	ヨウ、かがや-く	shine; sparkle; gleam; twinkle	耀
燿	ヨウ、かがや-く	shine	燿

10E 寺 BISMUTH

B		侍女	8A5
10E		じじょ	1|5

Growing plant, hand, regular use of hands, clerical work 寺
Pictograph of a kneeling woman 女

寺	ジ、てら	temple	10E
蒔	ジ、ま-く	sow (seeds)	蒔
女	ジョ、ニョ、ニョウ、おんな、め	woman	10E
汝	ジョ、なんじ	you; thou	汝

10F 語 BISMUTH

ℬ	語調	3C7	
10F	ごちょう	*	

Words + ngu character I/me (originally two identical reels) 語

五	ゴ、いつ、いつ-つ	five	10F
梧	ゴ、あおぎり	Chinese parasol tree; phoenix tree	梧
伍	ゴ、くみ	5; 5-man squad; file; line	伍
吾	ゴ、わ-が、われ	I; my; our; one's own	吾

10G 方 BISMUTH

ß	見方	12A20
10G	みかた	02|03

Possibly tethered boats in the current, square 方
Originally three tens, thirty years, one generation 世

方	ホウ、かた	side, way, square, direction, person	10G
於	オ、お-いて	at; in; on; as for	於
世	セイ、セ、よ	world, society, age, generation	10G
笹	ささ	bamboo grass	笹
貰	セイ、もら-う	get; have; obtain	貰

11A 仏 BLACK BRIMSTONE

ぁ	仏教	6C13
11A	ぶっきょう	*

Nose, self 仏

仏	ブツ、ほとけ	Buddha, France	11A

佛	VARIANT OF 仏	Buddha, France	佛
払	フツ、はら-う	pay, sweep away, rid	11A
拂	VARIANT OF 払	pay, sweep away, rid	拂
頌	ショウ	eulogy	頌

11B 才 BLACK BRIMSTONE

ᛞ	天才	4–2
11B	てんさい	6‖8

Originally dam across a stream 才
Pictograph of a tree 木
Originally showing a person with a large head, up, above 天

木	ボク、モク、き、こ	wood	11B
杏	アン、キョウ、あんず	apricot	杏
禾	カ、いね	2-branch tree	禾
宋	ソウ	dwell	宋
李	リ、すもも	plum	李
天	テン、あめ、あま	heaven, sky	11B

昊	コウ、そら	sky; big	昊
呑	ドン、の-む	drink	呑

11C 至 BLACK BRIMSTONE

☵	至らない	9B17
11C	いたらない	2|||10

Pictograph of an arrow falling to the ground 至
Birth/life and forehead, phonetically expressing birth/growth 産
Pictograph of a wine jar + liquid 酒

至	シ、いた-る	go, reach, peak	11C
渥	アク、あつ-い	kindness	渥
姪	テツ、おい、めい	niece	姪
産	サン、う-む、う-まれる、うぶ	birth, produce	11C
薩	サツ	Buddha	薩
酒	シュ、さけ、さか	alcohol, sake	11C
酉	ユウ、とり	west; bird; 5-7pm; tenth sign of Chinese zodiac; sake radical	酉

11D 止 BLACK BRIMSTONE

🔍	中止	3B13
11D	ちゅうし	*

Foot, stop, planting the foot 止

止	シ、と-まる、と-める	stop	11D
凪	なぎ	lull; calm	凪
渋	ジュウ、しぶ、しぶ-い、しぶ-る	hesitate, astringent	11D
澁	VARIANT OF 渋	hesitate, astringent	澁

11E 心 BLACK BRIMSTONE

🔍	愛国心	3C7
11E	あいこくしん	*

Pictograph of a heart 心

心	シン、こころ	heart, feelings	11E

応	オウ	respond, react	11E
應	Old form of 応	respond, react	應
雁	ガン、かり	wild goose	雁
鷹	ヨウ、たか	hawk	鷹

11F 行 BLACK BRIMSTONE

| ☠ | 運行 | 2–9 |
| 11F | うんこう | * |

Pictograph of crossroads 行

11G 羽 BLACK BRIMSTONE

| ☠ | 羽毛 | 5A12 |
| 11G | うもう | * |

Pictograph of bird's wings 羽

| 羽 | ウ、は、はね | wing, feather, bird counter | 11G |
| 摺 | ショウ、す-る | rub; fold; print (on cloth) | 摺 |

12A 外 BLOOD STONE

⊂	占い者	11F14
12A	うらないしゃ	1|1

BLOOD STONE: Synonym for gold

Crescent moon and divination (crack in turtle shell) 外
Originally showing something emerging from the mouth; exhaling and vocalising 呼

外	ガイ、ゲ、そと、ほか、はず-す、はず-れる	outside, other, undo	12A
貼	チョウ、テン、は-る	stick; paste; apply	12A
帖	ジョウ、チョウ	quire (of paper); bundle of seaweed; counter for screens; notebook	帖
砧	チン、きぬた	fulling block	砧
禎	テイ	happiness	禎
禎	VARIANT OF 禎	happiness	禎
鮎	デン、あゆ、	fresh water trout; smelt	鮎

	なまず		
卜	ボク、うらな-う	divining; fortune-telling	卜
呼	コ、よ-ぶ	call, breathe	12A
乎	コ、か、かな、や	question mark; ?	乎

12B 楽 BLOOD STONE

⊂		楽観的	2B7
12B		らっかんてき	*

Originally a type of oak whose leaves were eaten by silk worms 楽

楽	ガク、ラク、たの-しい、たの-しむ	pleasure, music	12B
樂	VARIANT OF 楽	pleasure, music	樂
薬	ヤク、くすり	medicine, drug	12B
藥	VARIANT OF 薬	medicine, drug	藥

12C 舌 BLOOD STONE

⊂	二枚舌	6A9
12C	にまいじた	*

Originally mouth + dry/forked thrusting weapon, phonetic emerge 舌

舌	ゼツ、した	tongue	12C
筈	カツ、はず	notch of an arrow; ought; must; should be; expected	筈

12D 周 BLOOD STONE

⊂	六百周	4A7
12D	ろっぴゃくしゅう	0|9

Originally field completely full of crops, complete, cycle 周

周	シュウ、まわ-り	circumference, around	12D
鯛	チョウ、たい	seabream; red snapper	鯛

12E 毎 BLOOD STONE

⊂	毎日	9I8
12E	まいにち	*

Plant and mother, fertility, richly growing plant 毎
Woman with nipples, suckling 母

母	ボ、はは	mother	12E
海	カイ、うみ	sea	12E
海	VARIANT OF 海	sea	海
悔	カイ、く-いる、く-やむ、くや-しい	regret, repent, vexed	12E
悔	VARIANT OF 悔	regret, repent, vexed	悔
晦	カイ、くら-い、みそか	dark; disappear	晦
梅	バイ、うめ	plum (fertility)	12E
梅	VARIANT OF 梅	plum (fertility)	梅
繁	ハン	profuse, rich, complex	12E
繁	VARIANT OF 繁	profuse, rich, complex	繁
敏	ビン	agile, quick, alert	12E

敏	VARIANT OF 敏	agile, quick, alert	敏
侮	ブ、あなど-る	scorn, despise	12E
侮	VARIANT OF 侮	scorn, despise	侮
苺	ボウ、いちご	strawberry	苺
毎	マイ	each, every	12E
毎	VARIANT OF 毎	each, every	毎

12F 筆 BLOOD STONE

⊂	筆者	4–5
12F	ひっしゃ	3|6

Hand holding brush 筆

Plant growth on a tree and/or wooden tablets bound together 葉

葉	ヨウ、は	leaf	12F
蝶	チョウ	butterfly	蝶
喋	チョウ、しゃべ-る	talk; chat; chatter	喋
牒	チョウ、ふだ	label; genealogy; circular	牒

12G 須 BLOOD STONE

⊂	必須	3F7
12G	ひっす	*

Head and attractive forehead, face 須

顔	ガン、かお	face	12G
叡	エイ、あき-らか、さと-い	intelligence	叡
頁	ケツ、ページ	page; leaf	頁
諺	ゲン、ことわざ	proverb	諺
彦	ゲン、ひこ	lad; boy (ancient)	彦
碩	セキ	large	碩
類	ルイ	resemble, variety, sort	12G
類	VARIANT OF 類	resemble, variety, sort	類

13A 孝 BORAX

⩊	孝行	3–1
13A	こうこう	*

Old man + child 孝

13B 氏 BORAX

⚘	氏名	7C14
13B	しめい	2|6

Originally ladle, now hill, prominent hilltop living 氏
Originally rice stored deep inside a building 奥

氏	シ、うじ	clan, family, Mr	13B
祇	ギ、シ、た-だ	national or local god; peaceful; great	祇
昏	コン、くら-い	dark; evening; dusk	昏
砥	シ、と-ぐ	whetstone; grindstone	砥
奥	オウ、おく	heart; interior	13B
奥	VARIANT OF 奥	heart, interior	奥
襖	オウ、ふすま	opaque sliding door	襖

13C 刀 BORAX

⚘	竹刀	4C17
13C	しない*	*

Curved sword, cut 刀

刀	トウ、かたな	sword	13C
籾	もみ	unhulled rice	籾
匁	もんめ	monme, weight, coin (3.75 grams)	匁
梁	リョウ、はり、やな	weir; fish trap; beam; girder	梁

13D 黒 BORAX

ᰔ		黒人	3D
13D		こくじん	*

Originally flame with window and marks of soot, black 黒

黒	コク、くろ、くろ-い	black	13D
黑	VARIANT OF 黒	black	黑
黛	タイ、まゆずみ	blackened eyebrows	黛
墨	ボク、すみ	ink, inkstick	13D
墨	VARIANT OF 墨	ink, inkstick	墨
黙	モク、だま-る	be silent	13D

| 默 | VARIANT OF 黙 | be silent | 黙 |

13E 通 BORAX

W	通勤	4B7
13E	つうきん	*

Chinese only raised, originally sun rising above a brushwood fence 通

通	ツウ、ツ、とお-る、とお-す、かよ-う	pass, way, commute	13E
桶	トウ、おけ	tub; bucket	桶
樋	トウ、とい、ひ	waterpipe; gutter; downspout; conduit	樋

13F 沿 BORAX

W	鉛筆	3
13F	えんぴつ	*

Hollowed out boat 沿

13G 夜 BORAX

⚛	夜明け	2–4
13G	よあけ	*

Clear moon 夜

14A 辛 BRICK

▥	辛苦	5A11
14A	しんく	0|6

Tattooist's needle, piercing, slaves, hardship, bitterness 辛

辛	シン、から-い	sharp, bitter	14A
梓	シ、あずさ	Catalpa tree	梓

14B 前 BRICK

▥	朝飯前	2A5
14B	あさめしまえ	*

Originally putting on one's clogs (hollowed out wood) and go 前

前	ゼン、まえ	before, front		14B

| 揃 | セン、そろ-う | be complete; uniform; all present | 揃 |

14C 台 BRICK

| IIIII | 台風 | 6B9 |
| 14C | たいふう | * |

Originally mound of earth on the top of which one is stationed 台

台	ダイ、タイ	platform, stand	14C
殆	タイ、あや-うい、ほとん-ど	almost; quite; really	殆
苔	タイ、こけ	moss; lichen	苔

14D 弟 BRICK

| IIIII | 弟子 | 4C4 |
| 14D 並 | でし | * |

Previously showing two and large, double large, supersize; fat 太
Set order in binding a stake (used as a weapon), sequence 弟

| 弟 | テイ、ダイ、デ、おと うと | younger brother | 14D |

悌 テイ	serving our elders	悌
鵜 テイ、う	cormorant	鵜
梯 テイ、はしご	ladder; stairs; insatiable drinking	梯

14E 妻 BRICK

ⅢⅢ	夫妻	8E14
14E	ふさい	*

Hand holding broom, house wife 妻

妻	サイ、つま	wife	14E
慧	エ、ケイ、さと-い	wise	慧
捷	ショウ、か-つ、はや-い	victory; fast	捷
寝	シン、ね-る、ね-かす	sleep, lie down	14E
寢	VARIANT OF 寝	sleep, lie down	寢
彗	スイ	comet	彗
棲	セイ、す、す-む	live; dwell	棲

14F 西 BRICK

IIIII	泰西	2E4
14F	たいせい	*

Originally basket, wine press 西

西	セイ、サイ、にし	west	14F
晒	サイ、さら-す	bleach; refine; expose; air	晒
栖	セイ、す-む	nest; rookery; hive; cobweb; den	栖
茜	セン、あかね	madder; red dye; turkey red	茜
粟	ゾク、あわ	millet	粟
栗	リツ、くり	chestnut	栗

14G 少 BRICK

IIIII	即妙	8B8
14G	そくみょう	*

Original meaning is "smaller than small", tiny size 少

少	ショウ、すく-ない、すこ-し	a little, few	14G
裟	サ、シャ	Buddhist surplice	裟
紗	サ、シャ、うすぎぬ	gauze; gossamer	紗

CHAPTER 3 GEMINI

15A 古 CALCINATION

Ⓡ	考古学	9D17
15A	こうこがく	*

Skull-like mask, ancestors, old 古

古	コ、ふる-い、ふる-す	old	15A
醐	ゴ	boiled butter	醐
瑚	ゴ	ancestral offering receptacle	瑚
胡	コ、えびす、なん-ぞ	barbarian; foreign	胡
糊	コ、のり	paste; glue; sizing	糊

15B 番 CALCINATION

ⓇR	順番	4E12
15B	じゅんばん	*

Rice plant + field, planting follows set order, roster, turn 番

番	バン	turn, number, guard	15B
悉	シツ、ことごと-く、つぶさ-に	all	悉
播	ハ、バン、ま-く	plant; sow	播
蕃	バン、えびす、しげ-る	grow luxuriously	蕃
幡	ハン、のぼり、はた	flag	幡
翻	ホン、ひるがえ-る、ひるがえ-す	flap, change	15B
飜	ALTERNATIVE OF 翻	flap, change	飜

15C 斤 CALCINATION

ⓡ	斤目	11C25
15C	きんめ	1‖4

Axe with shaped handle 斤
Original meaning is hill + growing plant, confusion with the character for commander 師

斤	キン	axe, weight	15C

祈	キ、いの-る	pray, hope	15C
祈	VARIANT OF 祈	pray, hope	祈
芹	キン、せり	parsley	芹
欣	キン、よろこ-ぶ	take pleasure in; rejoice	欣
師	シ	teacher, model, army	15C
獅	シ、しし	lion	獅

15D 市 CALCINATION

ⓡ	市場	4–7
15D	しじょう	*

Originally stop + confines + waterweed, levelling out of sell/buy 市

15E 形 CALCINATION

ⓡ	人形	4–4
15E	にんぎょう	*

Lattice window + hairs/pattern 形

15F 事 CALCINATION

Ⓡ	一事	4–2
15F	いちじ	*

Formerly hand and flag on a pole, identifying guild? Work, worker/servant 事

15G 谷 CALCINATION

Ⓡ	幽谷	7A10
15G	ゆうこく	*

Deeply, widely split opening, valley 谷

谷	コク、たに	valley, gorge	15G
蓉	ヨウ	lotus	蓉

16A 長 CAMPHOR

ⓍⓄ	長持ち	3B3
16A	ながもち	*

Originally showing an old man with flowing long hair 長

長	チョウ、なが-い	long, senior	16A
脹	チョウ	swell, bulge	脹
套	トウ	hackneyed	套

16B 京 CAMPHOR

| XO | 東京 | 8G8 |
| 16B | とうきょう | 0|2 |

House on a hill, noble 京
Original meaning is a prominent person arriving at a prominent house on the hill 就

京	キョウ、ケイ	capital	16B
鷲	シュウ、わし	eagle	鷲
尤	ユウ、とが-める、もっと-も	outstanding	尤
掠	リャク、かす.める、かす.る、かす.れる	pillage; rob; graze; skim; sweep over; cheat; hint	掠
亮	リョウ、あき-らか、すけ、まこと	clear; help	亮
涼	リョウ、すず-しい、すず-	cool	16B

	む		
涼	ALTERNATIVE OF 涼	cool	涼
諒	リョウ、まこと	fact; reality; understand; appreciate	諒
椋	リョウ、むくのき	type of deciduous tree; grey starling	椋

16C 高 CAMPHOR

XO	高最	2E8
16C	こうさい	*

Pictograph of a tall watchtower 高

高	コウ、たか-い、たか、たか-まる、たか-める	tall, high, sum	16C
膏	コウ、あぶら	fat; grease; lard; paste; ointment; plaster	膏
縞	コウ、しま	stripe	縞
塙	コウ、はなわ	projecting tableland or mountain	塙
藁	コウ、わら	straw	藁

嵩	スウ、かさ	be aggravated; grow worse; grow bulky; swell	嵩

16D 朝 CAMPHOR

xo	朝廷	4C3
16D	ちょうてい	*

Originally sun rising through plants, rise + river 朝

朝	チョウ、あさ	court, morning	16D
斡	アツ	go around; rule; administer	斡
戟	ゲキ、ほこ	halberd; arms	戟
廟	ビョウ、みたまや	mausoleum; shrine; palace	廟

16E 可 CAMPHOR

xo	可決	12C20
16E	かけつ	1|3

Mouth + twisting waterweed/ seek an exit 可

Mouth, meaning to tell + woman phonetically expressing to comply 如

可	カ	approve, can, should	16E
阿	ア、おもね-る	Africa; flatter; fawn upon; corner; nook; recess	阿
珂	カ	jewel	珂
綺	キ、あや	figured cloth; beautiful	綺
如	ジョ、ニョ	similar, equal	16E
恕	ジョ、ゆる-す	excuse	恕

16F 説 CAMPHOR

⚹	説得	10B8
16F	せっとく	0‖4

Mouth exhaling 只
Non General Use character exchange, barter, person dispersing words 説

説	セツ、ゼイ、と-く	preach, explain	16F
只	シ、た-だ	only	只
祝	シュク、シュウ、いわ-う	celebration	16F

祝	VARIANT OF 祝	celebration	祝

16G 直 CAMPHOR

xo	直立	8C3
16G	ちょくりつ	1|2

Eye + needle and corner, fix with direct piercing stare 直
Formerly dog and four mouths, mouths/receptacles have become the dominant meaning 器

直	チョク、ジキ、ただ-ちに、なお-す、なお-る	direct, upright, fix	16G
埴	ショク、はに	clay	埴
聴	チョウ、き.く、ゆる.す	listen (carefully)	16G
聽	VARIANT OF 聴	listen (carefully)	聽
徳	トク	virtue	16G
德	VARIANT OF 徳	virtue	德
器	キ、うつわ	vessel, utensil, skill	16G
器	VARIANT OF 器	vessel, utensil, skill	器

17A 門 CAPUT MORTUUM

Tm	表門	9B19
17A	おもてもん	*

Pictograph of a gate with a double door 門

門	モン、かど	gate, door	17A
閏	ジュン、うるう	intercalation; illegitimate throne	閏
閃	セン、ひらめ-く	flash; brandish	閃

17B 父 CAPUT MORTUUM

Tm	雷親父	2A1
17B	かみなりおやじ	*

Originally showing hand holding stick, rod of correction 父

父	フ、ちち	father	17B
斧	フ、おの	axe; hatchet	斧

17C 感 CAPUT MORTUUM

Tm	感情	3–10
17C	かんじょう	*

Chinese only unison, sharp weapon, trimming + mouth, all together 感

17D 風 CAPUT MORTUUM

Tm	一風	2B3
17D	いっぷう	*

Originally showing phoenix believed to ride the wind 風

風	フウ、フ、かぜ、かざ	wind, style	17D
颯	サツ	suddenly; smoothly	颯
楓	フウ、かえで	maple	楓

17E 泉 CAPUT MORTUUM

Tm	温泉	3–3
17E	おんせん	0|3

Pictograph of water emerging from a hole in a rock/hillside 泉

17F 矢 CAPUT MORTUUM

Tm	知合い	4A5
17F	しりあい	*

Pictograph of an arrow 矢

知	チ、しる	know	17F
智	チ、さと-い	wisdom; intellect; reason	智

17G 自 CAPUT MORTUUM

Tm	自然	3A
17G	しぜん	0|4

Nose, self 自

臭	シュウ、くさ-い	smell, smack	17G
臭	VARIANT OF 臭	smell, smack	臭

18A 且 CINNABAR

吉	且つ又	11C20

18A	かつまた	*

Pictograph of cairn, piled up stones on top of others 且.

且	か-つ	furthermore, besides	18A
誼	ギ、よし-み	friendship; intimacy	誼
畳	ジョウ、たた-む、たたみ	mat, size, fold, pile, repeat	18A
疊	VARIANT OF 畳	mat, size, fold, pile, repeat	疊
祖	ソ	ancestor	18A
祖	VARIANT OF 祖	ancestor	祖

18B 元 CINNABAR

ざ	元来	6A8
18B	がんらい	1|1

Person with the head exaggerated, upper part, prime part 元
Originally tree and "flame-like flowers", dazzling, shine 栄

元	ゲン、ガン、もと	originally, source	18B
莞	カン、いぐさ	reed used to cover tatami	莞

| 栄 | エイ、さか-える、は-え、は-える | flourish; prosperity; honour; glory; splendour | 18B |
| 榮 | VARIANT OF 栄 | flourish; prosperity; honour; glory; splendour | 榮 |

18C 介 CINNABAR

| ⚱ | 介入 | 2B5 |
| 18C | かいにゅう | * |

Casing, something in between, armour, shell 介

介	カイ	mediate, shell	18C
芥	カイ、あくた	mustard; rape; dust; trash; rubbish	芥
界	カイ	area, boundary	18C
堺	カイ、さかい	world	堺

18D 歩 CINNABAR

| ⚱ | 進歩 | 4C3 |
| 18D | しんぽ | * |

Originally doubling of foot, putting one foot in front of other 歩

歩	ホ、ブ、フ、ある-く、あゆ-む	walk	18D
歩	VARIANT OF 歩	walk	歩
渉	ショウ	cross over, liaise	18D
渉	VARIANT OF 渉	cross over, liaise	渉
瀕	ヒン	shore; brink; verge	瀕

18E 南 CINNABAR

| ☐ | 南極 | 2A3 |
| 18E | なんきょく | 0\|2 |

Warm side of the tent, south side? 南

| 南 | ナン、ナ、みなみ | south | 18E |
| 楠 | ナン、くすのき | Camphor tree | 楠 |

18F 予 CINNABAR

| ☐ | 預金 | 4A5 |

18F	よきん	*

Weaving shuttle pushed to one side, prior action 予

予	ヨ	already, prior, I	18F
野	ヤ、の	moor, wild	18F
埜	ALTERNATIVE OF 野	moor, wild	埜

18G 角 CINNABAR

	街角	4A8
18G	まちかど	0|1

Pictograph of a horn 角

角	カク、かど、つの	horn, angle	18G
蟹	カイ、かに	crab	蟹

19A 考 COPPER

	考案	2–1
19A	こうあん	*

Originally bent figure + long hair, twisting waterweed, old man 考

19B 半 COPPER

♀	半島	4A3
19B	はんとう	4‖6

Half a cow 半
Bird and mountain, islands in the sea where birds alight 島
Originally referring to offer to a high authority 奏

半	ハン、なか-ば	half, middle	19B
絆	ハン、きずな、ほだし	bonds; fetters	絆
島	トウ、しま	island	19B
嶋	ALTERNATIVE OF 島	island	嶋
奏	ソウ、かな-でる	play, present, report	19B
榛	シン、はしばみ、はんのき	hazelnut; filbert	榛
秦	シン、はた	Manchu Dynasty; name given to naturalized foreigners	秦
湊	ソウ、みなと	port; harbor	湊

19C 発 COPPER

♀	発表	2–7
19C	はっぴょう	*

Two planted feet shooting arrow from bow, dispatch 発

19D 豆 COPPER

♀	豆腐	10G29
19D	とうふ	*

Monopedal table-cum-food vessel with contents 豆

豆	トウ、ズ、まめ	beans, miniature	19D
凱	ガイ、やわ-らぐ	victory song	凱
鎧	ガイ、よろい	put on armour; arm oneself	鎧
葵	キ、あおい	hollyhock	葵
嬉	キ、うれ-しい	glad; pleased; rejoice	嬉
厨	チュウ、くりや	kitchen	厨
橙	トウ、だいだい	bitter orange	橙
逗	トウ、とど-まる	stop	逗

19E 平 COPPER

♀	平手	3A6
19E	ひらて	*

Twisting water weed, small, flat, 2 scales 平

平	ヘイ、ビョウ、たい-ら、ひら	flat, even, calm	19E
秤	ビン、はかり	balances; scales; steelyard	秤

19F 言 COPPER

♀	言回し	4A3
19F	いいまわし	*

Originally mouth and sharp: articulate? 言

言	ゲン、ゴン、い-う、こと	word, say, speak	19F
這	シャ、は-う	crawl; creep; grovel; trail (vines)	這

19G 走 COPPER

♀	奔走	4–3
19G	ほんそう	0‖14

Frantic movement with the foot, running 走

20A 亜 CORAL

↳	亜熱帯	2C8
20A	あねったい	0|2

Underground dwelling, crooked, hunchback 亜

亜	ア	next, sub-, Asia	20A
亞	VARIANT OF 亜	next, sub-, Asia	亞
悪	アク、オ、わる-い	bad, hate	20A
惡	VARIANT OF 悪	bad, hate	惡
淵	エン、ふち	abyss; edge; deep pool; the depths	淵

20B 主 CORAL

凵	主催	5A
20B	しゅさい	*

Originally ornately stemmed burning oil lamp, master 主

主	シュ、ス、ぬし、おも	master, owner, main	20B
註	チュウ	notes; comment; annotate	註

20C 身 CORAL

凵	身分	3–1
20C	みぶん	*

Miscopied body instead of bow and arrow 身

20D 秋 CORAL

凵	秋分	2B7
20D	しゅうぶん	*

Rice plant + fire, dry autumn crop-fires caused by Foehn 秋

| 秋 | シュウ、あき | autumn | 20D |

鍬	シュウ、くわ、すき	hoe with long blade at acute angle	鍬
萩	シュウ、はぎ	bush clover	萩

20E 衣 CORAL

		衣桁	6A5
20E 並		いこう	*

Originally showing collar and sleeves, clothing 衣
Combining the early form of clothing and fur, fur clothing, outside, surface 表

衣	イ、ころも	garment; clothes; dressing	20E
隈	ワイ、くま	corner	隈

20F 米 CORAL

		新米	3
20F		しんまい	*

Pictograph of a rice plant 米

20G 呂 CORAL

ㅂ	風呂	4–6
20G	ふろ	*

Former Jinmei character vertebrae, also joined blocks 呂

21A 死 CRUCIBLE

♡	早死に	2–5
21A	はやじに	*

Originally variant of meatless bone, death + person 死

21B 乗 CRUCIBLE

♡	乗り降り	4E2
21B 並	のりおり	0|1

Originally person on top of a tree, climb a tree, mount 乗
Building + woman, referring to a woman resting quietly during menses 安

乗	ジョウ、の-る、の-せる	ride, mount, load	21B
乗	VARIANT OF 乗	ride, mount, load	乗

剰	ジョウ	surplus, resides	21B
剩	VARIANT OF 剰	surplus, resides	剩
安	アン、やす-い	restful, ease, cheap	21B
按	アン	hold; consider; investigate	按
晏	アン、おそ-い、やす-い	late; quiet; sets (sun)	晏
鞍	アン、くら	saddle	鞍

21C 軍 CRUCIBLE

♈ 21C	空軍 くうぐん	4A8 *

Originally circle of carts, carts drawn into a circle, army 軍

軍	グン	military, army	21C
輝	キ、かがや-く	shine; light	輝

21D 与 CRUCIBLE

♈	与え主	2A4

| 21D | あたえぬし | * |

Originally four hands, many interlocking hands, joint effort 与

| 与 | ヨ、あた-える | give, convey, impart, involvement | 21D |
| 與 | VARIANT OF 与 | give, convey, impart, involvement | 與 |

21E 受 CRUCIBLE

| ♉ | 受付 | 3–3 |
| 21E | うけつけ | * |

Hand reaching down 受

21F 反 CRUCIBLE

| ♉ | 反応 | 8–3 |
| 21F | はんのう* | * |

Cliff, phonetic turn over + hand 反

21G 相 CRUCIBLE

| ♉ | 相談 | 4A7 |
| 21G | そうだん | 1|5 |

Eye watching from behind the tree, careful observation 相
Heart/feelings and brain, thoughts in the brain 思

相	ソウ、ショウ、あい	mutual, minister, aspect	21G
湘	ショウ	name of Chinese river; the Sagami river	湘
思	シ、おも-う	think	21G
偲	シ、しの-ぶ	recollect; remember	偲

CHAPTER 4 CANCER

22A 真 DAY

✦	真昼	4F7
22A	まひる	1|0

Originally person upside-down, (dead?), spirit, essence, truth 真
Originally indicating the bright section of the day 昼

真	シン、ま	true, quintessence	22A
眞	VARIANT OF 真	true, quintessence	眞
慎	シン、つつし-む	be discreet, refrain	22A
愼	VARIANT OF 慎	be discreet, refrain	愼
鎮	チン、しず-める、しず-まる	calm, suppress, weight	22A
鎭	VARIANT OF 鎮	calm, suppress, weight	鎭
顛	テン、いただき	overturn; summit; origin	顛
槙	テン、まき	twig; ornamental evergreen	槙
槇	VARIANT OF 槙	twig; ornamental evergreen	槇

| 昼 | チュウ、ひる | daytime, noon | 22A |
| 晝 | VARIANT OF 昼 | daytime, noon | 晝 |

22B 度 DAY

| ⊕ | | 程**度** | 2–1 |
| 22B | | ていど | * |

Measure various things with the hand, measurement 度

22C 列 DAY

| ⊕ | | **列**席 | 4A4 |
| 22C | | れっせき | 0\|1 |

Cut to the bone, set sequence for dismembering a carcass 列

| 列 | レツ | | row, line | 22C |
| 燦 | サン、きら-めく | | brilliant | 燦 |

22D 眼 DAY

| ⊕ | | 千里**眼** | 9–9 |

| 22D | せんりがん | 0\|5 |

Stop and stare, scrutinise (eye on legs) 眼

22E 旨 DAY

| ✧ | 趣旨 | 5–4 |
| 22E | しゅし | * |

Something sweet that is spooned into the mouth, lingering 旨

22F 皿 DAY

| ✧ | 灰皿 | 6C13 |
| 22F | はいざら | * |

Pictograph of a vessel 皿

皿	さら	dish, bowl, plate	22F
溢	イツ、あふ-れる	overflow; inundate; spill	溢
温	オン、あたた-か、あたた-かい、あたた-まる、あたた-める	warm	22F
溫	VARIANT OF 温	warm	溫
孟	モウ	chief; beginning	孟

22G 進 DAY

	進呈	12F22
22G	しんてい	1|1

Move with bird 進
Bamboo abacus 算

進	シン、すす-む、すす-める	advance	22G
惟	イ、おも-う、こ-れ、た-だ	consider; reflect; think	惟
雑	ザツ、ゾウ	miscellany	22G
雜	VARIANT OF 雑	miscellany	雜
雀	ジャク、すずめ	sparrow	雀
錐	スイ、きり	auger; drill; awl; pyramid; cone	錐
雛	スウ、ひな	chick; squab; duckling; doll	雛
碓	タイ、うす	pestle	碓
算	サン	calculate	22G
纂	サン、あつ-める	editing; compiling	纂

23A 丙 DECOCTION

⊕B	丙種	3–3
23A	へいしゅ	0|1

Large altar with sturdy legs 丙

23B 式 DECOCTION

⊕B	開会式	3–2
23B	かいかいしき	*

Carpenter's square and stake, measured intervals, order 式

23C 干 DECOCTION

⊕B	干潟	6B13
23C	ひがた	*

Forked thrusting weapon 干

干	カン、ほ-す、ひ-る	dry, defence	23C
竿	カン、さお	pole; rod; scale beam; violin neck	竿
栞	カン、しおり	bookmark	栞

23D 者 DECOCTION

耂	作者	10O15
23D	さくしゃ	2|3

Originally box for storing kindling, odds and ends, plebs 者
Originally showing two hands, two fires and rising smoke, brushwood on fire 蒸

者	シャ、もの	person	23D
者	VARIANT OF 者	person	者
煮	シャ、に-る、に-える、に-やす	boil, cook	23D
煮	VARIANT OF 煮	boil, cook	煮
署	ショ	government, office, sign	23D
署	VARIANT OF 署	government, office, sign	署
曙	ショ、あけぼの	dawn; daybreak	曙
暑	ショ、あつ-い	hot (weather)	23D
暑	VARIANT OF 暑	hot (weather)	暑
緒	ショ、チョ、お	beginning, cord, clue, connection	23D
緒	VARIANT OF 緒	beginning, cord, clue,	緒

		connection	
渚	ショ、なぎさ	strand; beach; shore	渚
渚	VARIANT OF 渚	strand; beach; shore	渚
諸	ショ、もろ	various, many	23D
諸	VARIANT OF 諸	various, many	諸
著	チョ、あらわ-す、いちじる-しい	notable, write book	23D
著	VARIANT OF 著	notable, write book	著
猪	チョ、い、いのこ	boar	猪
猪	VARIANT OF 猪	boar	猪
儲	チョ、もう-ける	be profitable; yield profit	儲
堵	ト、かき	fence; railing; enclosure	堵
都	ト、ツ、みやこ	capital, metropolis	23D
都	VARIANT OF 都	capital, metropolis	都
蒸	ジョウ、む-す、む-れる、む-らす	humid	23D
函	カン、はこ	box (archaic)	函
丞	ジョウ、ショウ、すく.う、	help	丞

	たす.ける	

23E 充 DECOCTION

⊞B	充分	6C6
23E	じゅうぶん	1‖1

New born baby with amniotic fluid 充
Old form indicates a spinning weight, rotating amongst people, convey 伝

流	リュウ、ル、なが-れる、なが-す	flow, stream	23E
侃	カン、つよ-い	strong; just; righteous; peace-loving	侃
疏	ソ、しる-す	estrangement; sparseness; neglect	疏
琉	リュウ、ル	lapis lazuli	琉
伝	デン、つた-わる、つた-える、つた-う	convey, transmit	23E
傳	VARIANT OF 伝	convey, transmit	傳

23F 求 DECOCTION

＋B	球広い	3A2
23F	たまひろい	*

Originally fur coat, desirable object 求

求	キュウ、もと-める	request, seek	23F
毬	キュウ、まり	burr; ball	毬

23G 路 DECOCTION

＋B	出演者	4B3
23G 並	しゅつえんしゃ	*

Descend, stop and start 路

Once written with foot and a line of containment, emerging foot 出

路	ロ、じ	road, route	23G
鷺	ロ、さぎ	heron	鷺
蕗	ロ、ふき	butterbur; bog rhubarb	蕗

24A 副 DIGEST

⼔	副業	4B6
24A	ふくぎょう	*

Chinese only full wine jar and altar, blessed by the gods, fortunate 副

福	フク	good fortune	24A
福	VARIANT OF 福	good fortune	福
富	フ、フウ、と-む、とみ	wealth, riches	24A
冨	ALTERNATIVE OF 富	wealth, riches	冨

24B 送 DIGEST

⼔	放送	6–4
24B	ほうそう	*

Royal we (Pluralis Majestatis) 送

24C 橋 DIGEST

⼔	陸橋	5C12
24C 並	りっきょう	*

Originally two horizontal lines indicating area below 下
Non General Use character tall, variant watchtower + person with bent neck, arched 橋

橋	キョウ、はし	bridge	24C
蕎	キョウ、そば	buck wheat	蕎
喬	キョウ、たか-い	high; boasting	喬
下	カ、ゲ、した、しも、もと、さ-げる、さ-がる、くだ-る、くだ-す、くだ-さる、お-ろす、お-りる	base, under, lower	24C
雫	しずく	drop; trickle; dripping	雫

24D 炎 DIGEST

一	気炎	3–4
24D	きえん	*

Double flame, excessive fire/heat 炎

24E 決 DIGEST

一	快楽	2A7

| 24E | かいらく | * |

Pulled apart by water 決

| 決 | ケツ、き-める、き-まる | decide, settle, collapse | 24E |
| 訣 | ケツ、わか-れる | separation; part; secret | 訣 |

24F 録 DIGEST

| 𠃍 | 記録 | 3D1 |
| 24F | きろく | * |

Liquid oozing from basket (from a crude wine press) 緑

緑	リョク、ロク、みどり	green	24F
綠	VARIANT OF 緑	green	綠
禄	ロク	fief; allowance; pension; grant; happiness	禄
祿	VARIANT OF 禄	fief; allowance; pension; grant; happiness	祿
録	ロク	record, inscribe	24F

錄 VARIANT OF 錄	record, inscribe		錄

24G 童 DIGEST

立	児**童**	4A5
24G	じどう	*

Slave standing on the ground carrying heavy sack 童

童	ドウ、わらべ	child	24G
撞	ドウ、つ-く	thrust; pierce; stab; prick	撞

25A 重 DISSOLUTION

⌑	**重**さ	6A3
25A	おもさ	*

Person standing on the ground carrying heavy sack 重

重	ジュウ、チョウ、え、おも-い、かさ-ねる、かさ-なる	heavy, pile, -fold	25A
董	トウ	correct	董

25B 員 DISSOLUTION

	吏員	5–2
25B	りいん	*

Originally round kettle, persons gathered around 員

25C 役 DISSOLUTION

	兵役	11C14
25C	へいえき	0|3

Strike with axe, phonetic throw 役

役	ヤク、エキ	role, service, duty	25C
毅	キ、たけ-し、つよ-い	strong	毅
繋	ケイ、か-かる、つな-ぐ	tie	繋
撃	ゲキ、う-つ	strike, attack, fire	25C
擊	VARIANT OF 撃	strike, attack, fire	擊

25D 幸 DISSOLUTION

	射幸	2A11

25D	しゃこう	*

Originally reversal of calamity, happiness 幸

幸	コウ、さいわ-い、さち、しあわ-せ	happiness, luck	25D
倖	コウ、こいねが-う、さいわ-い	happiness; luck	倖

25E 共 DISSOLUTION

🖥	洪水	6A7
25E	こうすい	*

Originally two hands offering a jewel, both, jointly together 共

共	キョウ、とも	together	25E
巷	コウ、ちまた	fork in road; scene; arena; theatre	巷

25F 錬 DISSOLUTION

🖥	錬金術	3E6
25F	れんきんじゅつ	*

Sack, bundle, disperse, threads soften by boiling 練

錬	レン	refine. train. drill	25F
鍊	VARIANT OF 錬	refine. train. drill	錬
蘭	ラン	orchid; Holland	蘭
欄	ラン	column. railing. space	25F
欄	VARIANT OF 欄	column. railing. space	欄
練	レン、ね-る	refine. knead. train	25F
練	VARIANT OF 練	refine. knead. train	練
煉	レン、ね-る	refine metals; kneading over fire	煉

25G 肖 DISSOLUTION

⌨	宵月	5D9
25G	よいずき	0|1

Flesh of the body + variant of little, phonetic resemble, kids 肖

肖	ショウ	be like, be lucky	25G
哨	ショウ	scout; sentinel	哨

梢	ショウ、こずえ	tree tops; twig	梢
鞘	ショウ、さや	sheath; case; margin; difference; shells (of beans)	鞘
屑	セツ、いさぎよ-い、くず	rubbish; junk; trash; waste; scraps	屑

26A 探 DISTILLATION

☞	探究者	2
26A	たんきゅうしゃ	*

Originally chimney-like hole, deep part of the river 探

26B 章 DISTILLATION

☞	憲章	3A4
26B	けんしょう	*

Tattooist's needle, identify slaves, mark, sign, badge 章

章	ショウ	badge, chapter	26B
樟	ショウ、くすのき	camphor	樟

26C 族 DISTILLATION

⌕	家族	5–7
26C	かぞく	*

Arrow under a streaming banner tied to a pole, mustering 族

26D 羊 DISTILLATION

⌕	羊飼い	9B17
26D	ひつじかい	*

Pictograph of a sheep 羊

羊	ヨウ、ひつじ	sheep	26D
祥	ショウ	good fortune, omen	26D
祥	VARIANT OF 祥	good fortune, omen	祥
翔	ショウ、か-ける	soar; fly	翔

26E 食 DISTILLATION

⌕	直 情 径 行	6–1
26E	ちょくじょうけいこう	1|2

Warp threads of the loom, incomplete, bare, light 径
Originally food in a long-stemmed dish, covered food in a dish 食

食	ショク、ジキ、く-う、く-らう、た-べる	food, eat	26E
喰	サン、く-う、く-らう	eat; drink; receive (a blow)	喰

26F 星 DISTILLATION

☙	出来星	2A4
26F	できぼし	*

Originally a trebling of sun and phonetic birth/life 星

星	セイ、ショウ、ほし	star	26F
悹	セイ、さと-い	realize	悹

26G 委 DISTILLATION

☙	国際捕鯨委員会	2A3
26G	こくさいほげいいいんかい	2|5

Rice plant and woman, pliable 委
Old form shows marked area and enclosed 国

委	イ	committee; entrust to; leave to; devote; discard	26G
倭	ワ、やまと	Yamato; ancient Japan	倭
摑	カク、つか-む	catch; seize; grasp; hold; arrest; capture	摑
国	コク、くに	country, region	26G
國	VARIANT OF 国	country, region	國

27A 穴 DRAGON'S BLOOD

🐉		穴埋め	4A2
27A		あなうめ	*

Space opened up in the ground and covered, dwelling, hole 穴

穴	ケツ、あな	hole	27A
突	トツ、つ-く	thrust, lunge, protrude	27A
突	VARIANT OF 突	thrust, lunge, protrude	突

27B 択 DRAGON'S BLOOD

ⓢ	選択	3A3
27B	せんたく	3|4

Originally take in hand and watch over file of prisoners, arrange 択
Originally expressing to follow someone along a road, movement + threads + together 選

択	タク	choose, select	27B
沢	タク、さわ	marsh, moisten, much, many, benefit	27B
皐	コウ	swamp; shore	皐
選	セン、えら-ぶ	elect; select; choose; prefer	27B
撰	セン、えら-ぶ	composing	撰
巽	ソン、たつみ	south east	巽
綴	テイ、テツ、つづ-る、と-じる	compose	綴

27C 灰 DRAGON'S BLOOD

ⓢ	灰塗れ	2B3

27C	はいまみれ	*

Formerly hand and fire: fire that one can hold in the hand? 灰

灰	カイ、はい	ashes	27C
恢	カイ	wide	恢
荻	テキ、おぎ	reed	荻

27D 面 DRAGON'S BLOOD

🐉	暗黒面	2–3
27D	あんこくめん	*

Formerly face and covering, that which covers the face, mask 面

27E 息 DRAGON'S BLOOD

🐉	休息	2–2
27E	きゅうそく	0|5

Nose + heart = essence of life, breathing air 息

27F 波 DRAGON'S BLOOD

🐉	波乗り	8A7

| 27F | なみのり | 1‖4 |

Hand pulling the hide of an animal with the head still attached 波
Attractive woman (plus sun) and house; bawdy house, revelry 宴

皮	ヒ、かわ	skin, leather	27F
頗	ハ、すこぶ-る	prejudiced; exceedingly	頗
宴	エン	banquet	27F
堰	エン、せき	dam; prevent; stop up	堰

27G 非 DRAGON'S BLOOD

| ⓢ | 非行 | 7B18 |
| 27G | ひこう | * |

Wings of a bird spreading apart as it is flies off 非

非	ヒ	not, un-, fault	27G
斐	ヒ	beautiful; patterned	斐
緋	ヒ、あか	scarlet; cardinal	緋

28A 去 DRAM

∆	過去	4A6
28A	かこ	*

Originally double lid on a rice container, consumption, gone? 去

去	キョ、コ、さ-る	go, leave, past	28A
劫	コウ、ゴウ、おびや-かす	threat; long ages	劫

28B 令 DRAM

∆	司令官	7F7
28B	しれいかん	*

Originally people summoned to hear the orders of their lord 令

令	レイ	order, rule	28B
玲	レイ	sound of jewels	玲
伶	レイ	actor	伶
怜	レイ、あわ-れむ、さと-い	wise	怜

羚	レイ、かもしか	antelope	羚
澪	レイ、みお	water route; shipping channel	澪
嶺	レイ、みね	peak; summit	嶺

28C 医 DRAM

⚠	産婦人科医	2B9
28C	さんふじんかい	*

Formerly expressing to attack with alcohol (arrow + quiver + strike + wine jar) 医

医	イ	doctor; medicine	28C
薙	テイ、な-ぐ	mow down (the enemy)	薙
俣	また	crotch	俣

28D 各 DRAM

⚠	各駅	10A15
28D	かくえき	2‖8

Descend, stop and start 各
Bringing shells/presents to the home 賓
Previously rain and three fields, repetition/reverberate 雷

各	カク、おのおの	each	28D
洛	ラク	Kyoto; the capital	洛
賓	ヒン	guest, visitor	28D
賓	VARIANT OF 賓	guest, visitor	賓
雷	ライ、かみなり	thunder	28D
蕾	ライ、つぼみ	bud (plants, mushrooms not yet opened)	蕾

28E 追 DRAM

| ⚘ | 追放 | 2A5 |
| 28E | ついほう | * |

Pair of buttocks, phonetic chase 追

| 追 | ツイ、お-う | chase, pursue | 28E |
| 槌 | ツイ、つち | hammer; mallet | 槌 |

28F 代 DRAM

⚠	部屋代	3–1
28F	へやだい	*

Person + stake, phonetic replace, stand-in, exchange 代

28G 振 DRAM

⚠	妊娠	7C10
28G	にんしん	0|1

Originally clam (now ngu character dragon) cutting grass, plants on field 振

振	シン、ふ-る、ふ-るう	wave, swing, air, manner, after	28G
晨	シン、あさ、あした	morning; early	晨
辰	シン、たつ	sign of the dragon; 7-9am; fifth sign of Chinese zodiac	辰
賑	シン、にぎ-わう	flourish; be bustling; prosperity	賑

CHAPTER 5 LEO

29A 祭 EARTH

▽	夏祭	4–1
29A	なつまつり	1|3

Hand placing meat on altar, worship 祭
Originally showing a person dancing with a mask 夏

夏	カ、ゲ、なつ	summer	29A
榎	カ、えのき	lotus tree	榎

29B 倍 EARTH

▽	倍加	6A4
29B	ばいか	*

Person and Chinese only spit 倍

倍	バイ	double, -fold	29B
菩	ボ、ほとけぐさ	kind of grass	菩

29C 然 EARTH

▽	燃焼	3–6
29C	ねんしょう	*

Roast dog meat 然

29D 欠 EARTH

▽	炊事	14B5
29D	すいじ	0‖4

Person yawning, wide open, vacant, lacking 欠

欠	ケツ、か-ける、か-く	lack	29D
欽	キン、うやま-う、つつし-む	respect; revere; long for	欽
盗	トウ、ぬす-む	steal	29D
盗	VARIANT OF 盗	steal	盗

29E 比 EARTH

⊽	比肩	9D21
29E	ひけん	1|1

People sitting next to each other 比
Originally tree, tributary, and sheep. Convoluted etymology 様

比	ヒ、くら-べる	compare, ratio	29E
匕	ビ	spoon	匕
琵	ビ	glissando on strings; lute	琵
庇	ヒ、かば-う、ひさし	protect; shield; defend; eaves; canopy; penthouse; visor	庇
毘	ヒ、ビ、たす-ける	help; assist	毘
様	ヨウ、さま	esq.; way; manner; situation; polite suffix	29E
樣	VARIANT OF 様	esq.; way; manner; situation; polite suffix	樣

29F 号 EARTH

⊽	番号	4B13

29F	ばんごう	*

Originally tiger's call 号
Big and emerge + words; boastful words 誇

号	ゴウ	number, call, sign	29F
誇	コ、ほこ-る	proud, boast	29F
袴	コ、はかま	men's formal divided skirt	袴
跨	コ、また-ぐ	be	跨

29G 有 EARTH

▽	所有者	6D9
29G	しょゆうしゃ	*

Originally right hand holding a piece of meat 有

有	ユウ、ウ、ある	have, exist	29G
郁	イク	cultural progress; perfume	郁
楕	ダ	ellipse	楕
侑	ユウ、すす-める、たす-ける	urge to eat	侑

| 宥 | ユウ、なだ-める、ゆる-す | soothe; calm; pacify | 宥 |

30A 基 EBULLITION

| ⚗ | 基礎 | 6D12 |
| 30A | きそ | * |

Non general use character "that", winnowing device, harvest, cycle of time 基

期	キ、ゴ	period, expect	30A
麒	キ	Chinese unicorn; genius; giraffe; bright; shining	麒
其	キ、そ-の、そ-れ	that	其
箕	キ、み	winnowing	箕
斯	シ、かか-る、ここ、こ-の、これ	this; thus; such; verbal pause	斯

30B 廷 EBULLITION

| ⚗ | 法廷 | 3A1 |

| 30B | ほうてい | * |

Chinese only artful, great, courtiers move to standing position on the ground 廷

| 廷 | テイ | court, government office | 30B |
| 挺 | チョウ、テイ | counter for guns, inksticks, palanquins, rickshaws; bravely volunteer | 挺 |

30C 成 EBULLITION

| 𣫅 | | 促成 | 4A1 |
| 30C | | そくせい | * |

Exact and trimming halberd 成

| 成 | セイ、ジョウ、な-る、な-す | become, make, consist | 30C |
| 晟 | セイ、あき-らか | clear | 晟 |

30D 官 EBULLITION

| 𣫅 | 警官 | 4A3 |

| 30D | けいかん | 0\|2 |

Roof + buttocks, phonetic work, sedentary activity 官

| 官 | カン | government, official | 30D |
| 菅 | カン、ケン、すげ | sedge | 菅 |

30E 永 EBULLITION

| ✿ | 永遠 | 3–4 |
| 30E | えいえん | 0\|2 |

Picture of the confluence of tributary and main river, originally long distance 永

30F 由 EBULLITION

| ✿ | 由縁 | 8D5 |
| 30F | ゆえん | * |

Basket/ wine press, drops falling from basket, cause 由

| 由 | ユ、ユウ、ユイ、よし | reason, means, way | 30F |
| 紬 | チュウ、つむぎ | pongee (a knotted silk cloth) | 紬 |

迪	テキ、みち	edify; way; path	迪
釉	ユウ、うわぐすり	glaze; enamel	釉
柚	ユウ、ゆず	citron	柚

30G 是 EBULLITION

| ✍ | 是正 | 4A5 |
| 30G | ぜせい | 0|1 |

Originally spoon kept on (proper) hook 是

| 是 | ゼ | proper, this | 30G |
| 醍 | ダイ | whey; good Buddhist teaching | 醍 |

31A 県 EFFERVESCENCE

| EF | 県庁 | 2A1 |
| 31A | けんちょう | * |

Originally joined threads/attach, severed head upside down in tree 県

| 県 | ケン | prefecture | 31A |
| 縣 | VARIANT OF 県 | prefecture | 縣 |

31B 具 EFFERVESCENCE

| EF | 台所道具 | 2A5 |
| 31B | だいどころどうぐ | * |

Originally showing hands holding up a kettle, offer a utensil 具

| 具 | グ | equip, means | 31B |
| 俱 | グ、とも-に、みな | both | 俱 |

31C 象 EFFERVESCENCE

| EF | 印象 | 2–1 |
| 31C | いんしょう | 0|1 |

Pictograph of an elephant 象

31D 迅 EFFERVESCENCE

| EF | 束の間 | 6–14 |

31D	つかのま	1‖4

Variant of east/tied sack with pole thrust through, bundle 束
Movement and element expressing fast 迅

迅	ジン	fast, intense	31D
訊	ジン、たず-ねる	request	訊

31E 免 EFFERVESCENCE

EF	逸品	4F12
31E	いっぴん	0|2

Women's genitals + crouching person, child birth, escape 免

免	メン、まぬか-れる	escape, avoid	31E
逸	イツ、そ.れる、そ.らす、はぐ.れる	escape, go astray, fast, excel	31E
逸	VARIANT OF 逸	escape, go astray, fast, excel	逸
兎	ト、うさぎ	rabbit; hare	兎
晩	バン	evening, late	31E
晩	VARIANT OF 晩	evening, late	晩

挽	バン、ひ-く	saw; turn (lathe); grind	挽
勉	ベン	strive	31E
勉	VARIANT OF 勉	strive	勉
娩	ベン	bear (children)	娩

31F 区 EFFERVESCENCE

EF	区別	5B13
31F	くべつ	*

Originally enclosure with three mouths, smaller enclosures Wards 区

区	ク	ward, section	31F
鴎	オウ、かもめ	seagull	鴎
駆	ク、か-ける、か-る	gallop, spur on	31F
駈	ALTERNATIVE OF 駆	gallop, spur on	駈

31G 及 EFFERVESCENCE

EF	及第点	4C3

31G	きゅうだいてん	*

Originally person + hand reaching out to seize 及

及	キュウ、およ-ぶ、およ-び、およ-ぼす	reach, extend, and	31G
笈	キュウ、おい	backpack bookcase	笈
汲	キュウ、く-む	draw (water); ladle; scoop; pump	汲
乃	ダイ、ナイ、すなわ-ち、の	from; possessive particle	乃

32A 央 ELEMENT

⊕	震央	3A7
32A	しんおう	*

Person with a yoke on the neck, restrained at the middle 央

英	エイ	superior, England	32A
瑛	エイ	sparkle of jewellery; crystal	瑛

32B 君 ELEMENT

₽	君主	3A5
32B	くんしゅ	*

Hand holding stick to govern and mouth 君

君	クン、きみ	lord, you, Mr	32B
伊	イ、こ-れ、た-だ	Italy	伊

32C 更 ELEMENT

₽	今更	4A4
32C	いまさら	*

Originally, enforce + third rate, enforced change of guard 更

更	コウ、さら、ふ-ける、ふ-かす	anew, change, again, grow late	32C
鞭	ベン、むち	whip; rod; counter for whippings	鞭

32D 昔 ELEMENT

㊐	今昔	6–3
32D	こんじゃく	*

Originally sun/day and piling up, accumulating, the past 昔

32E 宿 ELEMENT

㊐	宿題	2–2
32E	しゅくだい	*

Originally rush mat + building + person, resting 宿

32F 全 ELEMENT

㊐	安全	3–3
32F	あんぜん	0|2

Jewel under cover, precious, perfect, whole, complete 全

32G 不 ELEMENT

㊐	玉杯	3A6
32G	ぎょくはい	*

Pictograph of a calyx 不

杯	ハイ、さかずき	wine cup, cup (ful)	32G
盃	ALTERNATIVE FORM OF 杯	wine cup, cup (ful)	盃

33A 冬 EQUAL PARTS

dP	寒村	4A13
33A 並	かんそん	*

Old form phonetically expresses "become compact" and ice, winter 冬

Originally expressing binding of rushes to the wall of a house to insulate against cold 寒

冬	トウ、ふゆ	winter	33A
柊	シュウ、ひいらぎ	holly	柊

33B 建 EQUAL PARTS

dP	建物	3–1
33B	たてもの	*

Movement of an erect brush 建

33C 単 EQUAL PARTS

dP	簡単	5H12
33C	かんたん	*

Forked thrusting weapon 単

単	タン	simple, single, unit	33C
單	VARIANT OF 単	simple, single, unit	單
獣	ジュウ、けもの	beast	33C
獸	VARIANT OF 獣	beast	獸
禅	ゼン	meditation	33C
禪	VARIANT OF 禅	meditation	禪
戦	セン、いく-さ、たたか-う	fight, war	33C
戰	VARIANT OF 戦	fight, war	戰
蟬	セン、せみ	cicada	蟬
弾	ダン、ひ-く、はず-む、たま	bullet, spring, play	33C
彈	VARIANT OF 弾	bullet, spring, play	彈
箪	タン、わりご	bamboo rice basket	箪
畢	ヒツ、お-わる、ことごと-く	the end	畢

33D 帯 EQUAL PARTS

dP	熱帯魚	2B
33D	ねったいぎょ	0|1

Cloth and belt with items attached to it 帯

帯	タイ、お-びる、おび	wear, zone	33D
帶	VARIANT OF 帯	wear, zone	帶
滞	タイ、とどこお-る	stop, stagnate	33D
滯	VARIANT OF 滞	stop, stagnate	滯

33E 壮 EQUAL PARTS

dP	強壮	6D6
33E	きょうそう	*

Originally bed 爿 + samurai/male/ erect male organ 壮

壮	ソウ	manly, strong, grand, fertile	33E
壯	VARIANT OF 壮	manly, strong, grand, fertile	壯

荘	ソウ	villa, manor, solemn, majestic	33E
莊	VARIANT OF 荘	villa, manor, solemn, majestic	莊
装	ソウ、ショウ、よそお-う	wear, clothing, gear	33E
裝	VARIANT OF 装	wear, clothing, gear	裝
鼎	テイ、かなえ	three-legged kettle	鼎

33F 召 EQUAL PARTS

| dP | 大詔 | 8–7 |
| 33F | たいしょう | 0\|1 |

Mouth + person bending as they answer their master's summons 召

33G 井 EQUAL PARTS

| dP | 井戸 | 3–2 |
| 33G | いど | * |

Pictograph of a well 井

34A 害 ESSENCE

牛	殺害	3–2
34A	さつがい	*

Originally old (skull), inverted basket, cover head to smother? 害

34B 末 ESSENCE

牛	週末	2B2
34B	しゅうまつ	*

Tree with additional branches at the top, tip of tree 末

末	マツ、バツ、すえ	end, tip	34B
茉	マツ	jasmine	茉
沫	マツ、あわ、しぶき	splash; suds	沫

34C 幾 ESSENCE

牛	幾つ	3A2
34C	いくつ	1‖5

Short thread + variant of broad bladed halberd, loom 幾
Jinmei character originally expressing (emerging) plant 芝

幾	キ、いく	how many, how much	34C
磯	キ、いそ	seashore; beach	磯
芝	しば	lawn, turf	34C
之	シ、こ-の、これ、の、ゆ-く	this	之

34D 付 ESSENCE

付	仕付	5–9
34D	しつけ	*

Originally person + hand, reach out and give something to someone 付

34E 康 ESSENCE

康	健康体	2A1
34E	けんこうたい	*

Hands holding pestle pounding cereals 康

| 康 | コウ | peace, health | 34E |
| 傭 | ヨウ、やと-う | employ | 傭 |

34F 漢 ESSENCE

芇	漢字	6H7
34F	かんじ	*

Originally Han river gleaming like a flaming arrow 漢

漢	カン	Han China, man	34F
漢	VARIANT OF 漢	Han China, man	漢
勤	キン、ゴン、つと-める、つと-まる	work, duties	34F
勤	VARIANT OF 勤	work, duties	勤
菫	キン、すみれ	violet	菫
謹	キン、つつし-む	circumspect	34F
謹	VARIANT OF 謹	circumspect	謹
歎	タン、なげ-く	grief; lamentation	歎
嘆	タン、なげ-く、なげ-かわしい	lament, admire	34F
嘆	VARIANT OF 嘆	lament, admire	嘆
灘	タン、なだ	open sea	灘
難	ナン、かた-い、むずか-しい	difficult, trouble	34F

| 難 | VARIANT OF 難 | difficult, trouble | 難 |

34G 要 ESSENCE

半	重要	3–2
34G	じゅうよう	*

Originally two hands holding a waist, middle part, pivot, essential 要

35A 民 EXTRACTION

⇌	移民	3–4
35A	いみん	*

Needle in the eye, blind, slave, lowly people, commoners 民

35B 勢 EXTRACTION

⇌	勢力	4A4
35B	せいりょく	*

Kneeling to plant a tree 勢

| 勢 | セイ、いきお-い | power, force | 35B |

芸	ゲイ	art, skill, plant	35B
藝	VARIANT OF 芸	art, skill, plant	藝

35C 銭 EXTRACTION

⇨	金銭	6–13
35C	きんせん	*

Halberd cutting bone 浅

35D 即 EXTRACTION

⇨	即刻	2C
35D	そっこく	*

Originally taking one's place at the table, food + person 即

即	ソク	immediate, namely, accession	35D
卽	VARIANT OF 即	immediate, namely, accession	卽
櫛	シツ、くし	comb	櫛
節	セツ、セチ、ふし	section, joint, period, point, tune, restrain	35D
節	VARIANT OF 節	section, joint, period, point, tune, restrain	節

35E 暁 EXTRACTION

	暁星	2E13
35E	ぎょうせい	1|5

Chinese only high, trebling of earth 堯
Old form expresses dry and empty bowl, exhaust extended meaning 尽

暁	ギョウ、あかつき	dawn, light, event	35E
暁	VARIANT OF 暁	dawn, light, event	曉
驍	ギョウ	strong; good horse	驍
尭	ギョウ、たか-い	high; far	尭
堯	VARIANT OF 尭	high; far	堯
焼	ショウ、や-く、や-ける	burn, roast	35E
燒	VARIANT OF 焼	burn, roast	燒
尽	ジン、つ-くす、つ-きる、つ-かす	use up, exhaust	35E
盡	VARIANT OF 尽	use up, exhaust	盡

35F 川 EXTRACTION

⇨	川床	8C2
35F	かわどこ	3|0

Originally showing water flowing between two banks 川
Originally sandbank in a river, separate area, province 州
Right hand and mouth. Right hand indicates strength 右

川	セン、かわ	river	35F
馴	ジュン、な-れる	get used to; experienced; tamed	馴
釧	セン、くしろ	bracelet	釧
州	シュウ、す	province, sandbank	35F
洲	シュウ、す	continent; sandbar; island; country	洲
右	ウ、ユウ、みぎ	right	35F
佑	ユウ、たす-ける	help; assist	佑
祐	ユウ、たす-ける	help	祐
祐	VARIANT OF 祐	help	祐

35G 的 EXTRACTION

⇔	的外れ	4C4
35G	まとはずれ	*

White, conspicuous and pictograph of a ladle/scoop, setting apart, target 的

的	テキ、まと	target, like, adjectival suffix	35G
勺	シャク	ladle, measure	勺
灼	シャク、や-く	miraculous	灼
豹	ヒョウ	leopard; panther	豹

CHAPTER 6 VIRGO

36A 兆 FERMENTATION

🜛	前兆	6-6
36A	ぜんちょう	*

Cracks appearing on a heated turtle shell, divination 兆

36B 陸 FERMENTATION

🜛	陸海空	2–2
36B	りくかいくう	*

Hill and mound (Chinese only), land 陸

36C 戒 FERMENTATION

🜛	戒行	2–1
36C	かいぎょう	*

Two hands holding a halberd, threat, commanding, punishing 戒

36D 鏡 FERMENTATION

| 🜛 | 望遠鏡 | 2–1 |

| 36D | ぼうえんきょう | * |

Non general use character finish, sound + bent figure 境

36E 包 FERMENTATION

🀰	小包み	6A18
36E	こづつみ	0|4

Originally embryo in womb 包

包	ホウ、つつ-む	wrap, envelop	36E
鞄	ホウ、かばん	suitcase; bag; briefcase	鞄

36F 利 FERMENTATION

🀰	利益	3C7
36F	りえき	*

Reaping the harvest, pouring forth 利

利	リ、き-く	profit, gain, effect	36F
莉	リ	jasmine	莉
俐	リ、さと-い	clever	俐

黎	レイ、くろ.い	dark		黎

36G 鸛 FERMENTATION

𦥑	觀光	4–14
36G	かんこう	5‖5

Chinese only heron 鸛
Formerly depicting a variant of fire + bending person, fire carried overhead, torch? 光

光	コウ、ひか-る、ひかり	light, shine	36G
洸	コウ	sparkling water	洸
滉	コウ	deep and broad	滉
晃	コウ、あき-らか	clear	晃
晄	ALTERNATIVE FORM OF 晃	clear	晄
幌	コウ、ほろ	canopy; awning; hood; curtain	幌

37A 量 FILTRATION

33	重量	2
37A	じゅうりょう	*

Originally heavy sack left on the ground 量

37B 輪 FILTRATION

33	絶倫	6B11
37B	ぜつりんの	*

Chinese only arrange, align neatly (bamboo tablets bound together) 倫

輪	リン、わ	wheel, hoop	37B
珊	サン、サンチ	stagger; loneliness; centimetre	珊
綸	リン	thread; silk cloth	綸

37C 義 FILTRATION

33	意義	4–7
37C	いぎ	*

Sheep (praiseworthy) + I, consider oneself praiseworthy 義

37D 布 FILTRATION

33	絹布	6A2
37D	けんぷ	*

Hand beating cloth 布

布	フ、ぬの	cloth, spread	37D
凧	いかのぼり、たこ	kite	凧

37E 告 FERMENTATION

33	広告	3B7
37E	こうこく	*

Variant growing plant, phonetic proffer, proffer from the mouth 告

告	コク、つ-げる	proclaim, inform	37E
皓	コウ、しろ-い	white; clear	皓
浩	コウ、ひろ-い	wide expanse; abundance; vigorous	浩

37F 失 FILTRATION

33	失業	5–4
37F	しつぎょう	*

Originally lose by slipping from the hand 失

37G 変 FILTRATION

33	変遷	5A17
37G	へんせん	0|1

Originally Chinese only tied together, phonetic reverse 変

| 変 | ヘン、か-わる、か-える | change, strange | 37G |
| 亦 | エキ、ま-た | also; again | 亦 |

38A 争 FIRE

△	戦争	4C5
38A 並	せんそう	*

Hand reaching down to take hold of someone and restrain 争
Original representation of vapours rising from cooked rice 気

争	ソウ、あらそ-う	conflict, vie	38A
爭	VARIANT OF 争	conflict, vie	爭
浄	ジョウ	pure, clean	38A
淨	VARIANT OF 浄	pure, clean	淨
気	キ、ケ	spirit	38A
氣	VARIANT OF 気	spirit	氣

38B 以 FIRE

| △ | 以内 | 2–1 |
| 38B | いない | * |

Originally person behind a plough 以

38C 砕 FIRE

| △ | 砕氷 船 | 5D12 |
| 38C | さいひょうせん | 0|2 |

Marked clothing indicating slave or soldier 砕

| 砕 | サイ、くだ-く、くだ-ける | break, smash | 38C |

砕	VARIANT OF 砕	break, smash	砕
粋	スイ	pure, essence, style	38C
粋	VARIANT OF 粋	pure, essence, style	粋
翠	スイ、かわせみ、みどり	green	翠
酔	スイ、よ-う	drunk, dizzy	38C
酔	VARIANT OF 酔	drunk, dizzy	酔

38D 博 FIRE

△	博物館	5–10
38D	はくぶつかん	*

Spread, big, extensive 博

38E 奴 FIRE

△	奴隷	3–6
38E	どれい	*

Woman, compliance, work 奴

38F 良 FIRE

△	良心	6D8
38F	りょうしん	2|7

Originally sieve selecting the good 良
Phonetically expressing partner for a woman, husband 婿

良	リョウ、よ-い	good	38F
廊	ロウ	walk way	38F
廊	VARIANT OF 廊	walk way	廊
郎	ロウ	man, husband	38F
郎	VARIANT OF 郎	man, husband	郎
狼	ロウ、おおかみ	wolf	狼
朗	ロウ、ほが-らか	clear, fine, cheerful	38F
朗	VARIANT OF 朗	clear, fine, cheerful	朗
婿	セイ、むこ	son-in-law	38F
楚	ソ、いばら	whip	楚
疋	ヒキ、あし	head	疋

38G 航 FIRE

△	航空	3A4
38G	こうくう	*

Non general use character high, originally lashing boats together in a straight line 航

航	コウ	sail, voyage	38G
杭	コウ、くい	stake; post; picket	杭

39A 夫 FIRST MATTER

▽	夫君	5B6
39A 並	ふくん	*

Originally big male with an ornamental hairpin (sign of adulthood) 夫
Formerly mouth and standing person: person giving a verbal statement, presenting a report 呈

夫	フ、フウ、おっと	husband, man	39A
芙	フ	lotus; Mount Fuji	芙
呈	テイ	present, offer	39A

逞	テイ、たくま-しい	sturdy; brawny; bold	逞

39B 則 FIRST MATTER

▽	原則	3–3
39B	げんそく	*

Originally notches in a kettle, scale 則

39C 兵 FIRST MATTER

▽	兵器	2–2
39C	へいき	*

Axe being held with both hands 兵

39D 票 FIRST MATTER

▽	投票	3A8
39D	とうひょう	*

Originally leaping tongues of flame 票

票	ヒョウ	vote, label, sign	39D
瓢	ヒョウ、ひさご、ふくべ	gourd	瓢

39E 愛 FIRST MATTER

▽	渇愛	2–2
39E	かつあい	*

Previously enveloped heart, completely covered. (convoluted etymology) 愛

39F 旧 FIRST MATTER

▽	旧式	7D21
39F	きゅうしき	*

Originally crested bird with cry of 'kyuu', simplification 旧

旧	キュウ	old, past	39F
焔	エン、ほのお	flame; blaze	焔
陥	カン、おちい-る、おとしい-れる	collapse	39F
陷	VARIANT OF 陥	collapse	陷
児	ジ、ニ	child	39F
兒	VARIANT OF 児	child	兒
稲	トウ、いね、いな	rice (plant)	39F

稲	VARIANT OF 稲		rice (plant)	稲

39G 采 FIRST MATTER

⚗	喝采	4–1
39G	かっさい	*

Take/gather/pluck, hand + tree/shrub 采

40A 別 FIXATION

⚗	誘拐	2–2
40A	ゆうかい	*

Variant of bone 別

40B 林 FIXATION

⚗	林間	5F15
40B 並	りんかん	*

Ideograph of trees 林
Trail of rice plants in an ordered regularly spaced row 歴

林 リン、はやし	woods, forest	40B

彬	ヒン	refined; gentle	彬
焚	フン、た-く、や-く	burn; kindle; build a fire; boil; cook	焚
琳	リン	jewel; tinkling of jewellery	琳
淋	リン、さび-しい	lonely; deserted	淋
歴	レキ	history	40B
歷	VARIANT OF 歴	history	歷
暦	レキ、こよみ	calendar, almanac	40B
曆	VARIANT OF 暦	calendar, almanac	曆

40C 又 FIXATION

| ♇ | 最大 | 4A4 |
| 40C 並 | さいだい | * |

Originally warrior's helmet, attack + take 最
Originally pictograph of the right hand, again is borrowed meaning 又

| 又 | また | or again; furthermore; on the other hand | 40C |
| 叉 | サ、また | fork in road | 叉 |

40D 吉 FIXATION

	妥**結**	3A8
40D	だけつ	0|2

Originally double-lidded container, plenty, good fortune 吉

吉	キチ、キツ	good luck, joy	40D
桔	キツ	used in plant names	桔

40E 参 FIXATION

	参加	2–19
40E	さんか	*

Originally attractive woman, kneeling with three ornamental hairpins 参

40F 弓 FIXATION

	弓道	5B11
40F 並	きゅうどう	*

Pictograph of a bow 弓

Chinese only not and water binding being undone, disperse 沸

弓	キュウ、ゆみ	bow	40F
夷	イ、えびす、たい-らげる	barbarian	夷
穹	キュウ、キョウ、あめ、そら	sky	穹

40G 豚 FIXATION

| ♇ | 豚肉 | 7D17 |
| 40G | ぶたにく | 0\|1 |

Flesh and pig 豚

豚	トン、ぶた	pig, pork	40G
縁	エン、ふち	relation(s), ties, fate, edge	40G
緣	VARIANT OF 縁	relation(s), ties, fate, edge	緣
啄	タク、たた-く、ついば-む	peck; pick up	啄
琢	タク、みが-く	polish	琢
琢	VARIANT OF 琢	polish	琢

41A 牙 FLOWERS OF SATURN

万	象牙の塔	4B4
41A	ぞうげのとう	*

Former NGU character picturing interlocking fangs 牙

牙	ガ、ゲ、きば	tusk; fang	41A
冴	ゴ、こお-る、さ-える	be clear; serene; cold; skilful	冴
穿	セン、うが-つ	put on (to the feet); dig; pierce; drill	穿

41B 折 FLOWERS OF SATURN

万	折衷	5–1
41B	せっちゅう	*

Originally chop down trees, longstanding miscopy 折

41C 侯 FLOWERS OF SATURN

| 万 | 侯爵 | 3–2 |

| 41C | こうしゃく | 0‖2 |

Originally meet, greet, target range or archery 侯

41D 述 FLOWERS OF SATURN

ち	述語	4–5
41D 並	じゅつご	*

Originally entrance of a primitive dwelling 入
Originally hand with bits (of glutinous rice) sticking to it 述

41E 司 FLOWERS OF SATURN

ち	司会者	6–8
41E	しかいしゃ	*

Originally mirror image of anus, sedentary work? 司

41F 倹 FLOWERS OF SATURN

ち	倹約	5E14
41F	けんやく	*

Originally two talking persons examining horses, discuss 倹

| 倹 | ケン | thrifty, frugal | 41F |

儉	VARIANT OF 倹	thrifty, frugal	儉
検	ケン	investigate	41F
檢	VARIANT OF 検	investigate	檢
険	ケン、けわ-しい	steep, severe, perilous	41F
險	VARIANT OF 険	steep, severe, perilous	險
験	ケン、ゲン	examine	41F
驗	VARIANT OF 験	examine	驗
剣	ケン、つるぎ	sword, bayonet	41F
劍	VARIANT OF 剣	sword, bayonet	劍

41G 倉 FLOWERS OF SATURN

| 倉 | 創造 | 2B7 |
| 41G | そうぞう | * |

Cover, preserving + door, that which is covered behind a door 倉

| 倉 | ソウ、くら | warehouse, sudden | 41G |
| 蒼 | ソウ、あお-い | blue; pale | 蒼 |

| 槍 | ソウ、やり | spear; lance; javelin | 槍 |

42A 復 FURNACE

⊟	復習	5–5
42A	ふくしゅう	*

Chinese only go back, food Chinese only container of reversible shape + inversed foot 復

42B 果 FURNACE

⊟	果汁	6A7
42B	かじゅう	*

Originally fruit on a tree, replaced by rice field, abundant crop, outcome 果

果	カ、は-たす、は-てる、は-て	fruit, result, carry out	42B
巣	ソウ、す	nest	42B
巢	VARIANT OF 巣	nest	巢

42C 必 FURNACE

⊡	必然	5A4
42C	ひつぜん の	*

Originally halberd/lance between two poles (to prevent break) 必

必	ヒツ、かなら-ず	necessarily	42C
秘	ヒ、ひ-める	(keep) secret	42C
祕	VARIANT OF 秘	(keep) secret	祕

42D 志 FURNACE

⊡	意志	4–4
42D 並	いし	*

Pictograph of an extended finger 一
Emerging plant, movement of the heart, intent 志

42E 佳 FURNACE

⊡	絶佳	7E18
42E	ぜっか	*

Non general use character edge/angle/jewel, raised earthen paths 佳

佳	カ	beautiful, good	42E
娃	アイ	beautiful	娃
奎	ケイ	star; god of literature	奎
桂	ケイ、かつら	Japanese Judas-tree; Cinnamon tree	桂
圭	ケイ、かど、たま	square jewel; corner; angle; edge	圭
窪	ワ、くぼ-む	depression; cave in; sink; become hollow	窪

42F 加 FURNACE

⊟	添加	3G4
42F	てんか	*

Add strength to an argument by adding one's own words 加

加	カ、くわ-える、くわ-わる	add, join	42F
迦	カ	(used phonetically)	迦
珈	カ	ornamental hairpin	珈
駕	ガ	vehicle; palanquin; litter; hitch up an animal	駕

伽	カ、とぎ	nursing; attending; entertainer	伽
茄	カ、なす	eggplant	茄
嘉	カ、よ-い	applaud; praise; esteem	嘉
袈	ケ	a coarse camlet	袈

42G 胃 FURNACE

⊟	胃酸	3A12
42G	いさん	*

Pictograph of the stomach and (underneath) flesh of the body 胃

胃	イ	stomach	42G
謂	イ、い-う、おも-う	reason; origin; history; oral tradition	謂

CHAPTER 7 LIBRA

43A 居 GLASS

古	住居	3A2
43A	じゅうきょ	*

Slumped figure and old, so staying immobile, in one place 居

居	キョ、い-る	be, reside	43A
鋸	キョ、のこぎり	saw (tool)	鋸

43B 臣 GLASS

古	大臣	4D7
43B	だいじん	*

Eye, wide eyed alertness, guard, servant, subject 臣

臣	シン、ジン	retainer, subject	43B
臥	ガ、ふ-す、ふ-せる	bend down; bow; lie prostrate	臥

樫	かし	evergreen oak	樫
煕	キ	bright	煕
竪	ジュ、たて	length	竪

43C 勇 GLASS

古	蛮勇	2–1
43C	ばんゆう	*

Originally expressing break through and strength 勇

43D 易 GLASS

古	貿易	2A5
43D	ぼうえき	*

Originally big-eyed lizard + rays of the sun, iridescent, change 易

易	エキ、イ、やさ-しい	easy, change, divination	43D
錫	シャク、すず	copper; tin	錫

43E 妖 GLASS

古	妖精	5–4
43E	ようせい	*

Originally referred to a type of thistle (bamboo + person with bowed head) 妖

43F 尚 GLASS

古	高尚	8B19
43F	こうしょう	1|7

Originally smoke rising out of the window of a house, height 尚
Originally expressing to offer someone a valuable object, reward/praise in return 賛

賞	ショウ	prize, praise	43F
嘗	ショウ、ジョウ、かつ-て、な-める	once; before; formerly; ever; never; ex-; lick; lap up; burn up; taste; undergo; underrate; despise	嘗
裳	ショウ、も	skirt	裳
賛	サン	praise	43F
讃	サン、たた-える	praise; title on a picture	讃

43G 窓 GLASS

ざ	窓口	2A3
43G	まどぐち	*

Pictograph of a window with grille 窓

窓	ソウ、まど	window	43G
聡	ソウ、さと-い	wise; fast learner	聡

44A 墓 GLUE OF THE WISE

ざ	墓地	8A11
44A	ぼち	0‖4

Non general use character not, sun among many plants is setting, covered 墓

墓	ボ、はか	grave	44A
莫	バク、ボ、な-かれ	must not; do not; be not	莫

44B 亭 GLUE OF THE WISE

✎	料亭	2-1
44B	りょうてい	*

Simplification of tall, building + nail, phonetic stop/stay 亭

44C 協 GLUE OF THE WISE

✎	日本放送協会	3A1
44C	にっぽんほうそうきょうかい	*

Trebling of strength and ten, expressing many; strength of many persons, cooperate 協

協	キョウ	cooperate	44C
叶	キョウ、かな-う	grant	叶

44D 属 GLUE OF THE WISE

✎	付属	3A8
44D	ふぞく	*

Variant of tail + ngu character caterpillar 属

属	ゾク	belong, genus	44D
燭	ショク、ともしび	light	燭

44E 保 GLUE OF THE WISE

𝒮	保険	2–5
44E	ほけん	*

Originally mother carrying a child in a blanket 保

44F 責 GLUE OF THE WISE

𝒮	債権者	5A5
44F	さいけんしゃ	*

Taper, phonetic demand, money which can be demanded promptly 責

責	セキ、せ-める	liability, blame	44F
蹟	セキ、あと	remains; traces; footprint	蹟

44G 俊 GLUE OF THE WISE

♨	俊才	3D5
44G	しゅんさい	*

Chinese only linger/dawdle, stop/start + self and legs 俊

俊	シュン	excellence, genius	44G
允	イン	license	允
駿	シュン	a good horse; speed; a fast person	駿
竣	シュン、お-える	end; finish	竣
峻	シュン、けわ-しい、たか-い	high; steep	峻

45A 犯 GOLD

⚡	犯人	3–2
45A	はんにん	*

Pictograph of a slumped figure 犯

45B 片 GOLD

✍	片手	4–7
45B 並	かたて	*

Tree cut in half, thin piece 片
Formerly depicting an intricately patterned collar, (complex) writing 文

45C 那 GOLD

✍	旦那	2C6
45C 並	だんな	*

Specially interwoven cloth, rare 希
City where furs where worn, ancient barbarian kingdom 那

那	ナ	what?	45C
梛	ナ	type of tall evergreen tree	梛
希	キ	desire, hope for, rare	45C
稀	キ、ケ、まれ	rare; phenomenal; dilute (acid)	稀
肴	コウ、さかな	accompaniment for drinks	肴

45D 爆 GOLD

✏	爆発	2A1
45D	ばくはつ	*

Expose rice to the sun 爆

爆	バク	burst, explode	45D
曝	バク、あば-く、さら-す	bleach; refine; expose; air	曝

45E 修 GOLD

✏	悠然	4C6
45E 並	ゆうぜん	*

Brushing specks of dirt off clothes, elegant 修
Formerly hand striking person with a stick and tree, something straight, line 条

修	シュウ、シュ、おさ-める、おさ-まる	practice, master	45E
脩	シュウ、おさ-める	dried meat	脩
条	ジョウ	clause, item, line	45E

條	VARIANT OF 条	clause, item, line	條
篠	ショウ、しの	bamboo grass	篠

45F 貫 GOLD

⌀	貫通	2–1
45F	かんつう	*

Originally two shells/units of money threaded on a string 貫

45G 任 GOLD

⌀	妊婦	4A10
45G	にんぷ	*

Person + spindle, burden borne by a person, duty 任

任	ニン、まか-せる、まか-す	duty, entrust	45G
壬	ジン、みずのえ	9th calendar sign	壬

46A 示 GRADE OF FIRE

示	宗教	5F8

46A	しゅうきょう	1‖3

Altar with drops of blood/wine 示
Hand and thickly growing plant, religious offering from the forest 拜

示	ジ、シ、しめ-す	show	46A
祁	キ	intense	祁
綜	ソウ、す-べる	rule	綜
捺	ナ、ナツ、お-す	press; print; affix a seal; stamp	捺
凛	リン	cold	凛
凜	ALTERNATIVE OF 凛	cold	凜
廩	リン、ヒン、こめぐら	salary in rice	廩
拝	ハイ、おが-む	worship, respectful	46A
拜	VARIANT OF 拝	worship, respectful	拜

46B 築 GRADE OF FIRE

㝬	建築	2A3
46B	けんちく	*

Hand striking instrument 築

| 恐 | キョウ、おそ-れる、おそ-ろしい | fear, awe | 46B |
| 筑 | チク | ancient musical instrument | 筑 |

46C 矛 GRADE OF FIRE

| 孑 | 矛先 | 4A8 |
| 46C | ほこさき | * |

Barbed lance 矛

| 矛 | ム、ほこ | halberd, lance, spear | 46C |
| 茅 | ボウ、かや、ち | miscanthus reed | 茅 |

46D 鳥 GRADE OF FIRE

| 孑 | 候鳥 | 4C11 |
| 46D 並 | こうちょう | * |

Pictograph of a bird 鳥
Chinese only hawk, phonetic level, possibly settled on a level 隹

准	ジュン	level, conform, quasi-	46D
隼	ジュン、はやぶさ	falcon, hawk	隼
鳥	チョウ、とり	bird	46D
烏	オ、いず-くんぞ、からす	crow	烏
蔦	チョウ、つた	vine; ivy	蔦

46E 渦 GRADE OF FIRE

ず	渦巻き	4A4
46E	うずまき	*

Bone/vertebrae, flexibility, ease of movement 渦

渦	カ、うず	whirlpool, eddy	46E
禍	カ	calamity	46E
禍	VARIANT OF 禍	calamity	禍

46F 輸 GRADE OF FIRE

ず	輸出	4

| 46F | ゆしゅつ | * |

Chinese only affirmation, originally convey, boat + cap off, phonetic transfer 輸

46G 熊 GRADE OF FIRE

| ず | 大**熊**座 | 4–2 |
| 46G | おおぐまざ | 0\|1 |

Pictograph of a bear, ability "abearability" 熊

47A 禁 GRANATE

| 击 | **禁**煙 | 2–1 |
| 47A | きんえん | * |

Altar + forest phonetic. Abstain, abstain for religious reasons 禁

47B 規 GRANATE

| 击 | 規**制** | 2–1 |
| 47B | きせい | 2\|0 |

Originally prune a tree, order 制
Adult male and look, observe carefully, looked upon as a standard 規

規	キ	standard, measure	47B
窺	キ、うかが-う、のぞ-く	lie in wait	窺
槻	キ、つき	Zelkova tree	槻

47C 二 GRANATE

舌	武者	5A8
47C 並	むしゃ	*

Two fingers 二
Advance on foot with a halberd 武

二	ニ、ふた、ふた-つ	two	47C
竺	ジク	bamboo	竺

47D 余 GRANATE

舌	余暇	7A4
47D	よか	2|6

Cover + wooden cross frame, roomy ample 余
False + day, phonetically expressing space, day of leisure 暇

余	ヨ、あま-る、あま-す	excess, ample, I	47D
叙	ジョ	describe, confer	47D
敍	VARIANT OF 叙	describe, confer	敍
暇	カ、ひま	leisure, free time	47D
蝦	カ、えび	shrimp; prawn; lobster	蝦
霞	カ、かすみ	be hazy; grow dim; blurred	霞

47E 舎 GRANATE

舎	田舎	2–1
47E	いなか*	*

Originally mouth/breathe + ample, easily, relax 舎

47F 識 GRANATE

舎	常識	3–2
47F	じょうしき	*

The marker that produces words, intelligence, knowledge 識

47G 屯 GRANATE

	屯営	4A4
47G	とんえい	*

Originally sprouting plant + bud 屯

| 屯 | トン | barracks, camp, post | 47G |
| 沌 | トン | primeval chaos | 沌 |

48A 因 GUM

	因果 関係	4-3
48A	いんがかんけい	*

Big man + enclosure, prisoner, cause of imprisonment? 因

48B 牛 GUM

	耕作	5F14
48B 並	こうさく	*

Chinese only plough, or serrated wood 耕
Pictograph of a cow's head and horns 牛

牛	ギュウ、うし	cow	48B
牽	ケン、ひ-く	pull; tug; jerk; admit; install; quote; refer to	牽
犀	サイ	rhinoceros	犀
丑	チュウ、うし	sign of the ox or cow	丑
紐	チュウ、ひも	string	紐
眸	ボウ、ひとみ	pupil of the eye	眸
牟	ム	pupil (eye); moo (cow sound)	牟

48C 偉 GUM

5G	偉人	5B4
48C	いじん	*

Chinese only leather/hide, originally patrol, move all around 偉

偉	イ、えら-い	great, grand	48C
葦	イ、あし、よし	reed; bulrush	葦
衛	エイ	guard, protect	48C
衞	VARIANT OF 衛	guard, protect	衞

48D 曽 GUM

曽	僧院	6G2
48D	そういん	*

Originally build up, steam from a rice cooker 曽

曽	ソ、ソウ、かつ-て、すなわ-ち	formerly; once; before; ever; never; ex-	48D
曾	VARIANT OF 曽	formerly; once; before; ever; never; ex-	曾
噌	ソ、ソウ、かまびす-しい	boisterous	噌
僧	ソウ	priest	48D
僧	VARIANT OF 僧	priest	僧
層	ソウ	stratum, layer	48D
層	VARIANT OF 層	stratum, layer	層
贈	ゾウ、ソウ、おく-る	present, give	48D
贈	VARIANT OF 贈	present, give	贈
憎	ゾウ、にく-む、にく-い、にく-らしい、にく-しみ	hate(ful)	48D
憎	VARIANT OF 憎	hate(ful)	憎

増	ゾウ、ま-す、ふ-える、ふ-やす	increase, build up	48D
増	VARIANT OF 増	increase, build up	増

48E 綿 GUM

🐙	綿雪	2–3
48E	わたゆき	*

White, threads, and cloth/cotton 綿

48F 句 GUM

🐙	文句	7E18
48F	もんく	*

Mouth + cover/wrap/encircle, intertwining words, phrase 句
Plant and encircle + head of rice(plant), plant with a circular head 菊

句	く	phrase, clause	48F
絢	ケン、あや	kimono design	絢
詢	ジュン、はか-る、まこと	consult with	詢

179

洵	ジュン、まこと	alike; truth	洵
菊	キク	chrysanthemum	48F
掬	キク、すく-う	scoop up water with the hand	掬
鞠	キク、まり	ball	鞠

48G 逆 GUM

5G	遡行	5B7
48G	そこう	*

From inverted variant of big man, opposite normal, going backwards 逆

逆	ギャク、さか、さか-らう	reverse, oppose	48G
蕨	ケツ、わらび	bracken; fernbrake	蕨
朔	サク、ついたち	conjunction (astronomy); first day of month	朔

49A 災 GYPSUM

☿	災厄	2–19
49A	さいやく	1|13

Cliff, bending figure, danger 厄
Flood and Fire 災

災	サイ、わざわ-い	calamity	49A
勁	ケイ、つよ-い	strong	勁

49B 契 GYPSUM

☿	契約	3–5
49B	けいやく	0|1

Originally tally, right, proper 契

49C 券 GYPSUM

☿	拳銃	3–4
49C	けんじゅう	*

Originally expressing notched pledge 券

49D 雄 GYPSUM

♀	雄犬	6D11
49D	めすいぬ	1|4

Bird with forearm Chinese only, phonetic fine/showy bird, male bird 雄

Hands lifting together, rise 興

雄	ユウ、お、おす	male, powerful	49D
離	リ、はな-れる、はな-す	separate, leave	49D
禽	キン、とり	bird; captive; capture	禽
檎	ゴ	pear	檎
紘	コウ	large	紘
宏	コウ、ひろ-い	wide	宏
興	コウ、キョウ、おこ-る、おこ-す	rise, raise, interest	49D
輿	ヨ、こし	palanquin	輿

49E 豊 GYPSUM

♀	豊胸	2–6

| 49E | ほうきょう | * |

Originally showing food vessel and edible plant, full, plenty 豊

49F 講 GYPSUM

| 豆 | 講義 | 6–11 |
| 49F | こうぎ | 0\|3 |

Non general use character large amount, accumulation, two baskets piled up 講

49G 並 GYPSUM

| 豆 | 杉並木 | 4A3 |
| 49G | すぎなみき | 0\|1 |

Doubling of standing person, row/line, rank along side 並

| 並 | ヘイ、なみ、なら-べる、なら-ぶ、なら-びに | row, line, rank with, ordinary | 49G |
| 晋 | シン、すす-む | advance | 晋 |

CHAPTER 8 SCORPIO

50A 玄 HOUR

⊠	玄妙	11A10
50A	げんみょう	*

Short thread suitable for twisting, very small, hard to see 玄

玄	ゲン	occult, black	50A
絃	ゲン、いと	string; cord; samisen music	絃

50B 留 HOURS

⊠	留守番	4F15
50B	るすばん	*

Horse's bit, control 留

留	リュウ、ル、と-める、と-まる	stop, fasten	50B
卿	ケイ	you; lord; secretary; state minister	卿

昂	コウ、ゴウ、たか-い	rise	昂
卯	ボウ、う	sign of the hare or rabbit; 5-7am; fourth sign of Chinese zodiac; east	卯
昴	ボウ、すばる	The Pleiades	昴
劉	リュウ	axe; kill	劉
溜	リュウ、た-まる	collect; gather; be in arrears	溜

50C 忍 HOUR

✗	忍耐	2–2
50C	にんたい	*

Blade, phonetic bear, bear something painful in the heart? 忍

50D 刻 HOUR

✗	時刻	5A4
50D	じこく	*

Jinmei character zodiac hog, variant of pig, phonetic carve 刻

刻	コク、きざ-む	chop, mince, engrave	50D

| 亥 | ガイ、い | sign of the hog; 9-11pm; twelfth sign of the Chinese zodiac | 亥 |

50E 垂 HOUR

⊠	雨垂れ	4A2
50E	あまだれ	0‖3

Originally ground + plant with leaves hanging down to ground 垂

垂	スイ、た-れる、た-らす	suspend, hang down	50E
錘	スイ、つむ、おもり	spindle, sinker	錘

50F 護 HOUR

⊠	弁護士	3
50F	べんごし	*

Crested bird in hand, phonetic make dizzy, snare with words 護

50G 巻 HOUR

⊠	鉢巻	2D3

50G	はちまき	*

Hands rolling rice + curled or bent body 巻

巻	カン、ま-く、ま-き	roll, reel, volume	50G
巻	VARIANT OF 巻	roll, reel, volume	卷
圏	ケン	range, sphere, zone	50G
圏	VARIANT OF 圏	range, sphere, zone	圏
倦	ケン、あ-きる、う-む	lose interest in; tire of	倦
捲	ケン、ま-く	roll; wind; coil; turn pages; roll up sleeves; strip off; be turned; be rolled up	捲

51A 異 IRON

♛	異人	3–3
51A	いじん	*

Person putting on a mask, different, strange appearance 異

51B 編 IRON

♛	編集者	3A6
51B	へんしゅうしゃ	*

Originally doorplate, door + bound writing tablets 編

編	ヘン、あ-む	edit, knit, book	51B
篇	ヘン	volume; chapter; book; editing; compilation	篇

51C 域 IRON

♛	領域	7B16
51C	りょういき	*

Walk and halberd, originally walking one lap, Chinese only multiple of time 域

域	イキ	area, limits	51C
繊	セン	fine, slender	51C
纖	VARIANT OF 繊	fine, slender	纖
或	ワク、あ-る	some; one; or; possibly; ascertain	或

51D 宇 IRON

♛	宇頂天	3A13
51D	うちょうてん	*

Originally roof that completely covers, firmament/heaven 宇

宇	ウ	eaves, roof, heaven	51D
迂	ウ	roundabout way	迂

51E 煩 IRON

♛	煩悩	4–1
51E	ぼんのう	*

Person with exaggerated head 煩

51F 貴 IRON

♛	貴重	3–5
51F	きちょうな	*

Shell/money and non general use character gather, basket 貴

51G 監 IRON

⚓	監視	6A9
51G	かんし	*

Originally person bending over to stare at water in bowl 監

監	カン	supervise, watch	51G
覧	ラン	see, look	51G
覧	VARIANT OF 覧	see, look	覧

52A 男 JUNIPER

⚐	憂愁	2–1
52A	ゆうしゅう	1|3

Originally head/heart + upturned foot, walk slowly, phonetic sad 憂
Strength in the fields 男

男	ダン、ナン、おとこ	man, male	52A
甥	セイ、おい	nephew	甥

52B 適 JUNIPER

G	適性	5–2
52B	てきせい	*

Chinese only base/starting point, (emperor and mouth/say) 適

52C 敢 JUNIPER

G	勇敢	2C3
52C	ゆうかん	*

Originally pulling something out of a container, make-or-break effort? 敢

敢	カン	daring, tragic	52C
巌	ガン、いわお	rock; crag; boulder	巌
巖	VARIANT OF 巌	rock; crag; boulder	巖
厳	ゲン、ゴン、おごそ-か、きび-しい	severe, strict, solemn	52C
嚴	VARIANT OF 厳	severe, strict, solemn	嚴

52D 尺 JUNIPER

𝒢	尺八	4A3
52D	しゃくはち	0|2

Span of the hand, measure 尺

丈	ジョウ、たけ	length, stature, measure	52D
杖	ジョウ、つえ	staff; cane	杖

52E 将 JUNIPER

𝒢	将来	2D5
52E	しょうらい	*

Originally offer meat to a superior, (on a litter?) 将

将	ショウ	command, about to	52E
將	VARIANT OF 将	command, about to	將
奨	ショウ	urge, encourage	52E
奬	VARIANT OF 奨	urge, encourage	奬
醤	ショウ	a kind of miso	醬

| 蒋 | ショウ、ソウ、まこも、はげ.ます | reed | 蒋 |

52F 亡 JUNIPER

𝒢	文盲	7–9
52F	もんもう	*

Originally person no longer able to be seen, escaping 亡

52G 宅 JUNIPER

𝒢	自宅	2B2
52G	じたく	*

Roof and growing plant, 'taken root' 宅

宅	タク	house, home	52G
詫	タ、わ-びる	apologize	詫
托	タク	requesting; entrusting with; pretend; hint	托

53A 蔵 LEAD

カ	蔵書	2B
53A	ぞうしょ	*

Originally concealing a wounded + incapacitated person with grass 蔵

蔵	ゾウ、くら	storehouse, harbor	53A
藏	VARIANT OF 蔵	storehouse, harbor	藏
臓	ゾウ	entrails, viscera	53A
臟	VARIANT OF 臓	entrails, viscera	臟

53B 支 LEAD

カ	支店	7–5
53B	しじ	*

Hand holding up branch, originally break off a branch 支

53C 我 LEAD

カ	我まま	2B8
53C	わがまま	*

Originally broad bladed halberd with tassels, notches for kill 我

我	ガ、われ、わ	I, self, my	53C
峨	ガ	high mountain	峨
俄	ガ、にわ-か	sudden; abrupt; improvised	俄

53D 犬 LEAD

り		番犬	4A8
53D		ばんけん	*

Originally a pictograph of a dog on its hind legs barking 犬

犬	ケン、いぬ	dog	53D
状	ジョウ	condition, letter	53D
狀	VARIANT OF 状	condition, letter	狀

53E 尊 LEAD

り		尊敬	3E11
53E		そんけい	*

Offer and pour wine for a superior 尊

尊	ソン、たっと-い、とうと-い、たっと-ぶ、とうと-ぶ	value, esteem, your	53E
噂	ソン、うわさ	rumour; gossip; hearsay	噂
樽	ソン、たる	barrel; cask; keg	樽
鱒	ソン、ます	salmon; trout	鱒
鄭	テイ	an ancient Chinese province	鄭
楢	ユウ、なら	oak	楢

53F 善 LEAD

ｷｭ	親**善**	3–1
53F	しんぜん	*

Originally sheep + argue, praiseworthy argument, fine debate 善

53G 延 LEAD

ｷｭ	延期	2–5
53G	えんき	*

Lengthy protracted movement, foot + go and add mark 延

54A 匿 MAGNESIA

𝓜	匿名	3A1
54A	とくめい	*

Originally old person tending to long pliant hair, weak, young 匿

匿	トク	conceal	54A
惹	ジャク、ひ-く	attract; captivate	惹

54B 机 MAGNESIA

𝓜	事務机	4–3
54B	じむつくえ	*

Non general use character representing small table 机

54C 栽 MAGNESIA

𝓜	盆栽	3A
54C	ぼんさい	*

Fancy halberd cutting/trimming 栽

| 栽 | サイ | planting | 54C |
| 哉 | サイ、か、かな、や | how; what; alas; "?" | 哉 |

54D 座 MAGNESIA

| 𝓜 | 銀行口座 | 2B6 |
| 54D | ぎんこうこうざ | * |

Two persons sitting on the ground under a roof, gathering 座

座	ザ、すわ-る	seat, sit, gather	54D
坐	ザ、すわ-る、そぞ-ろに	sit	坐
巫	フ、みこ、かんなぎ	sorcerer; medium; shrine maiden	巫

54E 従 MAGNESIA

| 𝓜 | 従業員 | 2B4 |
| 54E | じゅうぎょういん | * |

Originally two persons moving along a road 従

従	ジュウ、ショウ、ジュ、したが-う、したが-える	follow, comply	54E
従	VARIANT OF 従	follow, comply	従
縦	ジュウ、たて	vertical, selfish	54E
縦	VARIANT OF 縦	vertical, selfish	縦

54F 株 MAGNESIA

| M | 株式会社 | 4–6 |
| 54F | かぶしきかいしゃ | * |

Originally inside of a tree trunk, often red 朱

54G 脳 MAGNESIA

| M | 頭脳 | 2–4 |
| 54G | ずのう | * |

Brain, hair, scoop, part of the head that is scooped out 脳

55A 斉 NIGHT

| X | 一斉 | 4A14 |

55A	いっせい	*

Similar heads of grain for religious offering 斉

斉	セイ	equal, similar	55A
齊	VARIANT OF 斉	equal, similar	齊

55B 操 NIGHT

✗	操縦士	4–6
55B	そうじゅうし	*

Chinese only birds chirping, three mouths in tree 操

55C 虛 NIGHT

✗	虛無主義	8E25
55C	きょむしゅぎ	0|11

Originally tiger, phonetic big, + large hill with a hollow crown 虛

虛	キョ、コ	empty, hollow, dip	55C
虛	VARIANT OF 虛	empty, hollow, dip	虛
戲	ギ、ゲ、たわむ.れる、た	play, frolic, joke	55C

	わむ.れ		
戯	VARIANT OF 戲	play, frolic, joke	戲
琥	コ	jewelled utensil	琥
彪	ヒョウ	spotted; mottled; patterned; small tiger	彪
虜	リョ	captive, capture	55C
虜	VARIANT OF 虜	captive, capture	虜

55D 専 NIGHT

✗	仁恵	3C4
55D	じんけい	*

Hand and round weighted device used in spinning 専

恵	ケイ、エ、めぐ-む	blessing, kindness	55D
惠	VARIANT OF 恵	blessing, kindness	惠
穂	スイ、ほ	ear, spear (of grain)	55D
穗	VARIANT OF 穂	ear, spear (of grain)	穗
専	セン、もっぱ-ら	exclusive, sole	55D

| 専 | VARIANT OF 専 | exclusive, sole | 専 |

55E 郷 NIGHT

✗	望郷	2B1
55E	ぼうきょう	*

Originally two persons meeting over dinner, feast, community 郷

郷	キョウ、ゴウ	village, rural	55E
饗	キョウ	banquet	饗
響	キョウ、ひび-く	resound, echo, effect	55E
響	VARIANT OF 響	resound, echo, effect	響

55F 革 NIGHT

✗	革命	3–4
55F	かくめい	*

Hornless creature with flaps of skin, hairless hide, change 革

55G 没 NIGHT

✕	陥没	3A4
55G	かんぼつ	*

Originally hand holding a gong to strike large hanging bell 没

没	ボツ	sink, disappear, die, lack, not	55G
穀	コク	grain, cereals	55G
穀	VARIANT OF 穀	grain, cereals	穀

56A 疑 OIL OF SATURN

疑	疑問	3–3
56A	ぎもん	*

Originally old man in doubt where to turn 疑

56B 垣 OIL OF SATURN

垣	宣伝	3E4
56B	せんでん	*

Originally that which goes around a building, wall, fence 垣

宣	セン	promulgate, state	56B
喧	ケン、かまびす-しい	noisy; boisterous	喧
萱	ケン、かや、わすれぐさ	miscanthus reed	萱
恒	コウ	always, constant	56B
恆	VARIANT OF 恒	always, constant	恆
亘	コウ、セン、わた-る	span; request	亘
亙	コウ、わた-る	range; reach; extend; cover	亙

56C 処 OIL OF SATURN

ק	処理	2–4
56C	しょり	*

Visiting somewhere and stop sitting on a stool 処

56D 且 OIL OF SATURN

ק	元且	4A5
56D	がんたん	*

Simplification of carry, former ngu character dawn, sun over the horizon 旦.

| 但 | ただ-し | but, however | 56D |
| 坦 | タン、たい-ら | level; wide | 坦 |

56E 滑 OIL OF SATURN

| ♑ | 潤滑 | 3–5 |
| 56E | じゅんかつ | * |

Skull and vertebrae, bones + flesh of the body 骨

56F 収 OIL OF SATURN

| ♑ | 収入 | 3B |
| 56F | しゅうにゅう | * |

Originally intertwined threads, assemble, gather 収.

収	シュウ、おさ-める、おさ-まる	obtain, store, supply	56F
收	VARIANT OF 収	obtain, store, supply	收
赳	キュウ	strong and brave	赳

56G 為 OIL OF SATURN

为	行為	2B1
56G	こうい	*

Originally hand + prototype elephant, imitate form, image 為

為	イ	do, purpose	56G
爲	VARIANT OF 為	do, purpose	爲
偽	ギ、いつわ-る、にせ	false, lie	56G
僞	VARIANT OF 偽	false, lie	僞

CHAPTER 9 SAGITTARIUS

57A 哀 PHILOSOPHICAL STONE

👑	悲哀	3–4
57A	ひあい	*

Mouth + clothing phonetic to express sound of wailing 哀

57B 補 PHILOSOPHICAL STONE

👑	補助	5E9
57B	ほじょ	*

Jinmei character begin, use + hand holding tool, start to use, phonetic patch 補

補	ホ、おぎな-う	make good, stop gap	57B
葡	ブ	wild grape; Portugal	葡
蒲	フ、ホ、がま	bulrush; flag; cattail	蒲
輔	ホ、たす-ける	help	輔
甫	ホ、はじ-め	for the first time; not until	甫

圃	ホ、はたけ	garden; field	圃

57C 享 PHILOSOPHICAL STONE

👑	享受者	4F9
57C	きょうじゅしゃ	1|8

Originally castle watchtower extending in two directions 享
Originally showing an old man leaning on a stick 老

享	キョウ	receive, have	57C
亨	キョウ、コウ、とお-る、に-る	undergo	亨
諄	ジュン	tedious	諄
淳	ジュン、あつ-い	pure	淳
醇	ジュン、あつ-い	pure sake	醇
惇	ジュン、トン、あつ-い	sincere	惇
敦	トン、あつ-い	industry	敦
老	ロウ、お-いる、ふ-ける	old, aged	57C
姥	ボ、うば	old woman	姥

57D 凶 PHILOSOPHICAL STONE

♛	凶悪	2–3
57D	きょうあくな	*

Container/mouth + symbol for drawing attention, empty 凶

57E 乳 PHILOSOPHICAL STONE

♛	乳房	4–9
57E	にゅうぼう	*

Originally manually assist in removing a child from the vagina 乳

57F 敬 PHILOSOPHICAL STONE

♛	敬称	3–1
57F	けいしょう	*

Non general use character insignificance, person bending, speaking respectfully 敬

57G 甲 PHILOSOPHICAL STONE

♛	甲虫	4A5
57G	こうちゅう	*

Hard-shelled seed with a split 甲

| 甲 | コウ、カン | shell, armour, high, 1st, A | 57G |
| 鴨 | オウ、あひる、かも | wild duck; easy mark | 鴨 |

58A 鬼 QUICKSILVER

☒	鬼界	5B10
58A	きかい	1|8

Person crouching wearing death mask, contact spirits dead 鬼
Old forms indicate plump thighs and penetration, "trading sex" 商

鬼	キ、おに	devil, demon, ghost	58A
魁	カイ、さきがけ	charging ahead of others	魁
蒐	シュウ、あつ-める	gather	蒐
商	ショウ、あきな-う	trade, deal, sell	58A
橘	キツ、たちばな	mandarin orange	橘

58B 刺 QUICKSILVER

☒	名刺	2–4

| 58B | めいし | * |

Non general use character thorn, (tree/wood + tapering), phonetic beat 刺

58C 声 QUICKSILVER

| ☿ | 暖炉 | 4–3 |
| 58C | だんろ | 1\|3 |

Former ngu character at this point, originally draw up (hand down, up + rope) 暖

Formerly a pictograph showing the striking of a musical instrument to produce a sound 声

| 声 | セイ、ショウ、こえ、こわ | voice | 58C |
| 馨 | ケイ、かお-る、かぐわ-しい | fragrant; balmy; favourable | 馨 |

58D 岡 QUICKSILVER

| ☿ | 静岡 | 4–3 |
| 58D | しずおか | * |

Former ngu character hill, hill + net, draw in/up, formidable hill, phonetic strong 岡

58E 奉 QUICKSILVER

☿	棒紅	3A
58E	ぼうべに	*

Originally two hands offering thickly growing plant, offer 奉

奉	ホウ、ブ、たてまつ-る	offer, respectful	58E
捧	ホウ、ささ-げる	lift up; give; offer; consecrate; sacrifice; dedicate	捧

58F 誤 QUICKSILVER

☿	誤解	4–2
58F	ごかい	*

Originally mouth/say + man with head tilted, bragging 誤

58G 陵 QUICKSILVER

☿	丘陵	3–2
58G	きゅうりょう	5|2

Originally two hills 丘

Originally high hill, mound 陵

陵	リョウ、みさぎ	imperial tomb, mound	53G
崚	リョウ	towering in a row	崚
綾	リョウ、あや	design; figured cloth; twill	綾
稜	リョウ、かど	angle; edge; corner; power; majesty	稜
凌	リョウ、しの-ぐ	endure	凌
菱	リョウ、ひし	diamond (shape); water chestnut; rhombus	菱

59A 既 QUINTESSENCE

⽆	慨嘆	3A12
59A	がいたん	*

Chinese only not without, person kneeling with head turned, unable 既

| 既 | キ、すで-に | already, finished | 59A |
| 厩 | キュウ、うまや | barn | 厩 |

59B 尉 QUINTESSENCE

🈔	小尉	2–2
59B	しょい	*

Press down with something hot, ironing, put into shape 尉

59C 茂 QUINTESSENCE

🈔	繁茂	3A5
59C	はんも	*

Pictograph of halberd/battle axe 茂

茂	モ、しげ-る	grow thickly	59C
戊	ボ、つちのえ	5th calendar sign	戊

59D 隠 QUINTESSENCE

🈔	雲隠れ	3–2
59D	くもがくれ	*

Chinese only compassion, care 隠

59E 激 QUINTESSENCE

✇	憤激	2–13
59E	ふんげき	*

Water, release (literally strike a person) and white, phonetic to beat, water striking 傲

59F 唐 QUINTESSENCE

✇	唐本	2–2
59F	とうほん	*

Originally mouth + hands holding pestle, phonetic brag/boast 唐

59G 甘 QUINTESSENCE

✇	甘え	7B18
59G	あまえ	0|2

Originally something held in the mouth, savoured, sweet 甘

甘	カン、あま-い、あま-える、-あま-やかす	sweet, presume upon	59G
柑	カン	citrus; orange	柑
湛	タン、たた-える	fill; wear (a smile)	湛

60A 患 RECTIFICATION

🏴	患者 家族	2
60A	かんじゃかぞく	*

Pierced heart, afflicted 患

60B 喝 RECTIFICATION

🏴	喝さい	7C13
60B	かっさい	*

Chinese only range of interrogatives, say, encircle, surround and person: ask and/or threaten 喝

喝	カツ	shout, scold	60B
謁	エツ	audience (with ruler)	60B
謁	VARIANT OF 謁	audience (with ruler)	謁
渇	カツ、かわ-く	thirst, parched	60B
渇	VARIANT OF 渇	thirst, parched	渇
掲	ケイ、かか-げる	display, hoist, print	60B
掲	VARIANT OF 掲	display, hoist, print	掲

60C 懐 RECTIFICATION

🏳	壊滅	2B
60C	かいめつ	*

Wrap Chinese only conceal/carry in the sleeve, eye, variant of multitude 懐

壊	カイ、こわ-す、こわ-れる	break, destroy, ruin	60C
壞	VARIANT OF 壊	break, destroy, ruin	壞
懐	カイ、ふところ、なつ-かしい、なつ-かしむ、なつ-く、なつ-ける	bosom, yearn, fond	60C
懷	VARIANT OF 懐	bosom, yearn, fond	懷

60D 卸 RECTIFICATION

🏳	卸売	2-2
60D	おろしうり	*

Originally drive a cart 卸

60E 喚 RECTIFICATION

🚩	叫喚	2–5
60E	きょうかん	*

Chinese only lively, women's genitals + spread thighs with hands, sex 喚

60F 融 RECTIFICATION

🚩	金融	2–3
60F	きんゆう	*

Large pot on stand 隔

60G 兼 RECTIFICATION

🚩	兼用	5A5
60G	けんよう	1|1

Originally hand holding two rice plants, doing two things at once 兼
Original character expressing trader, items that are being traded 価

兼	ケン、か-ねる	combine, unable	60G
簾	レン、すだれ	bamboo screen; rattan blind	簾
価	カ、あたい	price, value, worth	60G

價 VARIANT OF 価	price, value, worth	價

61A 挟 SAL-AMMONIAC

✹ 61A	板**挟**み いたばさみ	4C10 *

Non general use character insert, big person squeezed between two others 挾

挟 キョウ、はさ-む、はさ-まる	insert, pinch, squeeze between	61A
峡 キョウ	ravine, gorge	61A
峽 VARIANT OF 峡	ravine, gorge	峽
俠 キョウ、きゃん、おとこだて	tomboy; chivalry	俠
狭 キョウ、せま-い、せば-める、せば-まる	narrow, small	61A
狹 VARIANT OF 狭	narrow, small	狹

61B 巨 SAL-AMMONIAC

✻	巨人	3A5
61B	きょじん	*

Carpenter's square characterised by its large size 巨

巨	キョ	huge, giant	61B
矩	ク、さしがね	ruler; carpenter's square	矩

61C 乙 SAL-AMMONIAC

✻	乙に	3A3
61C	おつに	*

Double bladed sword, unusual 乙

乙	オツ	odd, B, 2nd, stylish	61C
迄	キツ、まで	until; up to; as far as; to the extent	迄

61D 仰 SAL-AMMONIAC

✻	信仰	3

| 61D | しんこう | * |

Chinese only raise, bending person looking up respectfully 仰

61E 屈 SAL-AMMONIAC

| ✻ | 窮屈 | 4–2 |
| 61E | きゅうくつ | 0\|1 |

Originally tail/genitals, testes, put out/remove balls, castrate 屈

61F 缶 SAL-AMMONIAC

| ✻ | 缶切り | 3A7 |
| 61F | かんきり | * |

Secure vessel for pouring liquid into 缶

| 缶 | カン | can, boiler | 61F |
| 萄 | ドウ | grapevine; wild grape | 萄 |

61G 孤 SAL-AMMONIAC

| ✻ | 孤立 | 2A6 |
| 61G | こりつ | * |

Non general use character melon, phonetic alone 孤

孤	コ	orphan, lonely	61G
瓜	カ、うり	melon	瓜

62A 偶 SILVER

⚠	偶然	4A4
62A	ぐうぜん	*

Chinese only begin, not clear/open, scorpion with twisting tail 偶

偶	グウ	by chance, spouse, doll	62A
寓	グウ、よ-る	temporary abode; keep; imply; suggest	寓

62B 堅 SILVER

⚠	堅固	3–3
62B	けんご	*

Chinese only hard and wise, hand presses the eye? 堅

62C 傑 SILVER

会	豪**傑**	5D7
62C	ごうけつ	1|1

Chinese only bird's roost, heroic 傑
Originally referring to pig with (tall) fearsome sword-like weapons, wild boar 豪

傑	ケツ	outstanding	62C
舜	シュン	type of morning glory; Rose of Sharon; Althea	舜
麟	リン	Chinese unicorn; genius; giraffe; bright; shining	麟
鱗	リン、うろこ	scales (fish)	鱗
憐	レン、あわ-れむ	pity; have mercy; sympathise; compassion	憐
豪	ゴウ	strength, splendour, Australia	62C
壕	ゴウ、ほり	trench; dugout; air raid shelter	壕

62D 雲 SILVER

会	相合**傘**	4A5

62D 並	あいあいがさ	*

Pictograph of a parasol 傘
Originally billowing vapours, later used to speak + rain 雲

傘	サン、かさ	umbrella, parasol	62D
雲	ウン、くも	cloud	62D
云	ウン、い-う	say	云

62E 華 SILVER

☲	慶弔	5–11
62E	けいちょう	2|03

Deer, love and goodness 慶
Originally showing a plant with many leaves coming into bud 華

華	カ、ケ、はな	splendid, magnificent	62E
樺	カ、かば	birch	樺
嘩	カ、かまびす-しい	noisy	嘩

62F 需 SILVER

⛰	需要	4C15
62F	じゅよう	3‖05

Non general use character however, originally beard, beard soaked by the rain 需

Originally a pictograph of a pestle, borrowed to express middle of the day 午

Originally expressing a person, held in place (for a long time) 久

需	ジュ	need, demand	62F
而	ジ、しか-して、しこ-うして、なんじ	rake	而
濡	ジュ、ぬ-れる	get wet; damp; make love	濡
瑞	ズイ、みず	congratulations	瑞
午	ゴ	noon	62F
杵	ショ、きね	wooden pestle	杵
久	キュウ、ク、ひさ-しい	long time; old story	62F
灸	キュウ	moxa cautery; chastisement	灸
玖	キュウ	beautiful black jewel; nine	玖

62G 雇 SILVER

仌	回顧	2
62G	かいこ	*

Bird + door, ungainly flapping of a quail 雇

63A 頃 TIN

亻	日頃	2–3
63A	ひごろ	*

Character indicates slumped head, person fallen to one side 頃

63B 執 TIN

亻	執着	2–3
63B	しゅうちゃく	*

Old form shows shackles + kneeling person, shackle a prisoner, seize 執

63C 舟 TIN

亻	渡し舟	6A14
63C	わたしぶね	*

Boat 舟

舟	シュウ、ふね、ふな	boat	63C
磐	バン、いわ	rock; crag; cliff; wall (in a mine)	磐

63D 薫 TIN

✿		薫香	2B4
63D		くんこう	*

Pleasant smelling smoke 薫

薫	クン、かお-る	aroma, fragrance, aura	63D
薫	VARIANT OF 薫	aroma, fragrance, aura	薫
勲	クン	merit	63D
勲	VARIANT OF 勲	merit	勲

63E 渓 TIN

✿		渓谷	2A4
63E		けいこく	*

Originally valley + Chinese only 'doubt' twisting threads 渓

渓	ケイ	valley, gorge	63E
鶏	ケイ、にわとり	chicken, hen, cock	63E
鷄	VARIANT OF 鶏	chicken, hen, cock	鶏

63F 譲 TIN

| ᅛ | 互譲 | 4E7 |
| 63F | ごじょう | 0\|3 |

Originally people accusing each other 譲

譲	ジョウ、ゆず-る	hand over, yield	63F
讓	VARIANT OF 譲	hand over, yield	譲
嬢	ジョウ	young lady, daughter	63F
孃	VARIANT OF 嬢	young lady, daughter	嬢
醸	ジョウ、かも-す	brew, cause	63F
釀	VARIANT OF 醸	brew, cause	醸
穣	ジョウ、みの-る、ゆた-か	good crops; prosperity	穣
穰	VARIANT OF 穣	good crops; prosperity	穣

63G 企 TIN

🐾	企て	2A
63G	くわだて	*

Person + foot, phonetic precarious, standing on tiptoe 企

企	キ、くわだ-てる	plan, undertake	63G
祉	シ	well-being, happiness	63G
祉	VARIANT OF 祉	well-being, happiness	祉

CHAPTER 10 CAPRICORN

64A 荒 VITRIOL

🔑	荒れ狂う	2–3
64A	あれくるう	*

Chinese only vast watery waste, (river + death) 荒

64B 膝 VITRIOL

🔑	諸膝	2
64B	もろひざ	*

Tree + drops of moisture, resin, sap of the lacquer-tree 漆

64C 竜 VITRIOL

🔑	竜巻	4C9
64C	たつまき	*

Dragon, fearsome, flying 竜

竜	リュウ	dragon	64C
龍	VARIANT OF 竜	dragon	龍

滝	たき	cascade, waterfall	64C
瀧	VARIANT OF 滝	cascade, waterfall	瀧
寵	チョウ	affection; love; patronage	寵

64D 顕 VITRIOL

⚷	顕微鏡	2B1
64D	けんびきょう	*

Chinese only motes, small particles of dust, sunlight + double thread 顕

顕	ケン	manifest, visible	64D
顯	VARIANT OF 顕	manifest, visible	顯
湿	シツ、しめ-る、しめ-す	damp, moist, humid	64D
濕	VARIANT OF 湿	damp, moist, humid	濕

64E 秀 VITRIOL

⚷	誘惑	3–7
64E	ゆうわく	*

Rice plant + bending person, rice plant bent (heavy head), excellent 秀

64F 珍 VITRIOL

⌾	珍奇	5–9
64F 並	ちんき	*

Jewel and person + hair, phonetic pure/unblemished: rare 珍
Originally pictograph of the roots of a tree, essence/origin 本

64G 升 VITRIOL

⌾	升目	3–2
64G	ますめ	*

Ladle 升

65A 寿 WATER

▽	寿命	2D11
65A	じゅみょう	*

Originally old man who has lived a long time 寿

| 寿 | ジュ、ことぶき | long life, congratulation | 65A |
| 壽 | VARIANT OF 寿 | long life, congratulation | 壽 |

鋳	チュウ、い-る	cast, found, mint	65A
鑄	VARIANT OF 鋳	cast, found, mint	鑄
祷	トウ、いの-る	pray	祷
禱	VARIANT OF 祷	pray	禱

65B 叔 WATER

▽	叔父	5–5
65B	おじ	*

Originally hand pulling up a potato 叔

65C 盾 WATER

▽	後盾	2B1
65C	うしろだて	0|1

Eye + shield and possibly piercing/intently 盾

盾	ジュン、たて	shield, pretext	65C
楯	ジュン、たて	shield; buckler; pretext	楯
遁	トン、のが-れる	flee; escape; shirk; evade; set free	遁

65D 雌 WATER

▽	雌牛	2D8
65D	めうし	*

Non general use character this/here, foot/stop + sitting person 雌

雌	シ、め、めす	female	65D
些	サ、いささ-か	a little bit; sometimes	些
柴	サイ、しば	brush; firewood	柴
砦	サイ、とりで	fort; stronghold; entrenchments	砦
此	シ、か-く、ここ、こ-の、これ	this; current; next; coming; last; past	此

65E 崩 WATER

▽	山崩れ	2B4
65E	やまくずれ	*

String of matching jewels, matching join 崩

崩	ホウ、くず-れる、くず-す	crumble, collapse	65E
鵬	ホウ、おおとり	phoenix	鵬
朋	ホウ、とも	companion	朋

65F 頼 WATER

▽		瀬戸	2C6
65F		せと	*

Originally bundle, money, slash/cut, profit financially 頼

瀬	せ	shallows, rapids	65F
瀬	VARIANT OF 瀬	shallows, rapids	瀬
漱	ソウ、くちすす-ぐ	gargle; rinse mouth	漱
頼	ライ、たの-む、たの-もしい、たよ-る	request, rely	65F
賴	VARIANT OF 頼	request, rely	賴

65G 隻 WATER

▽		三隻	2–5

| 65G | さんせき | 0\|1 |

Bird and hand, one of a pair, as opposed to a pair 隻

66A 帝 WHITE LEAD

| ⚡ | 帝国 | 3A5 |
| 66A | ていこく | 0\|1 |

Two-tier table + cross-struts and item, variant of altar 帝

| 帝 | テイ | emperor | 66A |
| 蹄 | テイ、ひづめ | hoof | 蹄 |

66B 卓 WHITE LEAD

| ⚡ | 食卓 | 4–12 |
| 66B 並 | しょくたく | * |

Core meaning high/excellent 卓
Sun and one line cutting another representing cutting/opening, sun breaking through 早

66C 逮 WHITE LEAD

| ⚡ | 逮捕 | 2B9 |

| 66C | たいほ | * |

Originally seizing an animal by the tail 逮

逮	タイ	chase, seize	66C
庚	コウ、かのえ	7th; 7th calendar sign	庚
繡	シュウ、ぬいとり	sew; figured cloth	繡

66D 庶 WHITE LEAD

| ⊿ | 庶民 | 2A4 |
| 66D | しょみん | * |

Originally put things on a fire, many things 庶

| 庶 | ショ | multitude, various, illegitimate | 66D |
| 廿 | ジュウ | twenty | 廿 |

66E 尼 WHITE LEAD

| ⊿ | 尼寺 | 6A5 |
| 66E | あまでら | * |

Two slumped figures, phonetically 'ni' of 'bikuni', Sanskrit nun 尼

| 尼 | ニ、あま | nun, priestess | 66E |
| 梶 | ビ、かじ | sculling oar | 梶 |

66F 円 WHITE LEAD

| ｓ | 両替え | 2–2 |
| 66F | りょうがえ | 1\|2 |

Two persons speaking, having an 'exchange' 替
Old form indicates roundness + round kettle, circle 円

| 円 | エン、まる-い | round, yen | 66F |
| 圓 | VARIANT OF 円 | round, yen | 圓 |

66G 捜 WHITE LEAD

| ｓ | 捜索隊 | 2B6 |
| 66G | そうさくたい | * |

Originally searching for something by torchlight in a building 捜

捜	ソウ、さが-す	search; seek; investigate	66G
捜	VARIANT OF 捜	search; seek; investigate	捜
痩	ソウ、や-せる	get thin	66G
痩	VARIANT OF 痩	get thin	痩

67A 縄 WINE

✡		縄目	3B18
67A		なわめ	*

Thread and pictograph of a tadpole 縄

縄	ジョウ、なわ	rope, cord	67A
陀	ダ	steep	陀
舵	ダ、かじ	rudder; helm; wheel	舵

67B 棟 WINE

✡		病棟	3
67B		びょうとう	*

Originally raised earthen path around a field, raised, exposed 棟

67C 伐 WINE

❣	征伐	2A5
67C	せいばつ	*

Halberd cutting down 伐

伐	バツ	attack, cut down	67C
鳶	エン、とび	black kite; fireman; hook	鳶

67D 焦 WINE

❣	黒焦げ	2A2
67D	くろこげ	*

Bird roasting over a fire, scorching, charring, fretting 焦

焦	ショウ、こ-げる、こ-がす、こ-がれる、あせ-る	scorch, fret	67D
蕉	ショウ		banana	蕉

67E 苗 WINE

ⱽ	苗字	3–1
67E	みょうじ	*

Plants still in the field, not ready yet for cropping 苗

67F 徴 WINE

ⱽ	特徴	3C3
67F	とくちょう	*

Core meaning small, secretive 徴

徴	チョウ、しるし	sign, summon, levy	67F
徵	VARIANT OF 徴	sign, summon, levy	徴
徽	キ、しるし	good	徽
懲	チョウ、こ-りる、こ-らす、こ-らしめる	chastise, learn	67F
懲	VARIANT OF 懲	chastise, learn	懲

67G 沈 WINE

ⱽ	消沈	2A4

| 67G | しょうちん | * |

Originally hanging down in water, to sink 沈

| 沈 | チン、しず-む、しず-める | sink | 67G |
| 耽 | タン、ふけ-る | addicted | 耽 |

68A 幣 YEAR

| ～ | 弊害 | 3A5 |
| 68A | へいがい | * |

Cutting up by hand of small bits of cloth, offerings to gods 幣

| 幣 | ヘイ | offering, money | 68A |
| 瞥 | ベツ、み-る | glance at | 瞥 |

68B 凡 YEAR

| ～ | 平凡 | 3–2 |
| 68B | へいぼん | * |

Wind cloth, sail 凡

68C 峰 YEAR

～	主峰	3D3
68C	しゅほう	*

Chinese only butt, gore, in Chinese only compounds sharp 峰

峰	ホウ、みね	peak, top	68C
峯	ALTERNATIVE OF 峰	peak, top	峯
逢	ホウ、あ-う	meeting; tryst; date; rendezvous	逢
鋒	ホウ、きっさき	dagger; sword's point; festival car; float	鋒
蓬	ホウ、よもぎ	sagebrush; wormwood; mugwort	蓬

68D 曹 YEAR

～	軍曹	3A1
68D	ぐんそう	*

Originally two well matched people, (doubling of east/sack) 曹

曹	ソウ	official, companion	68D

| 漕 | ソウ、こ-ぐ | rowing; skull; paddle | 漕 |

68E 某 YEAR

〰	媒介	3A1
68E	ばいかい	*

Sweet produce of certain trees 某

| 某 | ボウ | a certain-, some- | 68E |
| 煤 | バイ、すす | soot; smoke-dried | 煤 |

68F 卑 YEAR

〰	卑劣	2B10
68F	ひれつ	*

Originally hand holding a wine-pressing basket, the last drops 卑

| 卑 | ヒ、いや-しい、いや-しむ、いや-しめる | lowly, mean, despise | 68F |
| 卑 | VARIANT OF 卑 | lowly, mean, despise | 卑 |

| 碑 | ヒ | tombstone, monument | 68F |
| 碑 | VARIANT OF 碑 | tombstone, monument | 碑 |

68G 徹 YEAR

| ぐ | 徹夜 | 2–1 |
| 68G | てつや | * |

Originally remove pot from a stand, remove clear 徹

69A 僕 YELLOW AMBER

| ぶ | 公僕 | 3–4 |
| 69A | こうぼく | * |

Originally slave carrying chamber-pot and turds, rough 僕

69B 揺 YELLOW AMBER

| ぶ | 揺り いす | 2E4 |
| 69B | ゆりいす | * |

Unclear swaying meat vessel 揺

| 揺 | ヨウ、ゆ-れる、ゆ-る、ゆ-らぐ、ゆ-る | shake, swing, | 69B |

	ぐ、ゆ-する、ゆ-さぶる、ゆ-すぶる	rock	
搖 VARIANT OF 揺		shake, swing	搖
謡	ヨウ、うたい、うた-う	Noh chant, song	69B
謠 VARIANT OF 謡		Noh chant, song	謠
瑶	ヨウ、たま	beautiful as a jewel	瑶
遥	ヨウ、はる-か	far off; distant; long ago	遥
遙 VARIANT OF 遥		far off; distant; long ago	遙

69C 冒 YELLOW AMBER

る	冒険	2–4
69C	ぼうけん	*

Protective helmet worn over the eyes, fighting man 冒

69D 慢 YELLOW AMBER

る	腕自慢	4C15
69D 並	うでじまん	*

Non general use character full/expansive 慢
Old form shows pot for steaming rice and lid, come together 会

慢	マン	lazy, rude, boastful	69D
蔓	マン、つる	vine; tendril; influence; connections; good offices; spread; sprawl; thrive; rampant; powerful	蔓
会	カイ、エ、あ-う	meet	69D
桧	カイ、ひのき、ひ	Japanese cypress	桧
檜	カイ、ひのき、ひ	Japanese cypress	檜

69E 避 YELLOW AMBER

| ろ | 避妊 | 4–16 |
| 69E | ひにん | * |

Buttocks, opening, needle, anal penetration 避

69F 噴 YELLOW AMBER

| ろ | 噴水 | 3–2 |

69F	ふんすい	*

Make a 'pon' sound with the mouth 噴

69G 抜 YELLOW AMBER

ろ	手**抜**かり	2B7
69G	てぬうかり	1|2

Obscure element dog, phonetic extract 抜
Originally beat hemp with sticks to make clothes, pulverise 散

抜	バツ、ぬ-く、ぬ-ける、ぬ-かす、ぬ-かる	pluck, extract, miss	69G
拔	VARIANT OF 抜	pluck, extract, miss	拔
髪	ハツ、かみ	hair	69G
髮	VARIANT OF 髪	hair	髮
散	サン、ち-る、ち-らす、ち-らかす、ち-らかる	scatter; disperse; spend; squander	69G
撒	サン、ま-く	scatter; sprinkle; give them the slip	撒

70A 寮 ZINC

丮	寮生	4B6
70A	りょうせい	*

Chinese only fuel used in sacrifices 尞

寮	リョウ	hostel, dormitory	70A
燎	リョウ、かがりび	burn; bonfire	燎
遼	リョウ、はる-か	distant	遼

70B 累 ZINC

丮	累計	2B8
70B	るいけい	*

Originally three fields suggesting build up, accumulation 累

累	ルイ	accumulate, involve	70B
螺	ラ、にな	small edible helical fresh-water mollusc	螺
塁	ルイ	fort, baseball, base	70B
壘	VARIANT OF 塁	fort, baseball, base	壘

70C 腕 ZINC

ヲ	手腕家	3C5
70C	しゅわんか	*

Originally straighten a bent body, display of strength 腕

腕	ワン、うで	arm, skill	70C
苑	エン、その	garden; farm; park	苑
椀	ワン	wooden or lacquered bowl	椀
碗	ワン	bay, gulf, porcelain bowl, teacup	碗

70D 励 ZINC

ヲ	策励	2–8
70D	さくれい	*

Formerly showing a scorpion, phonetically expressing to strive 励

70E 併 ZINC

ヲ	併用	5–11

| 70E | へいよう | * |

Non general character put together, two persons and matching stakes 併

70F 麻 ZINC

| 乍 | 麻薬 | 4A7 |
| 70F | まやく | * |

Originally cloth plant, hemp, flax 麻

| 麻 | マ、あさ | hemp, flax, numb | 70F |
| 麿 | まろ | I; you | 麿 |

70G 戻 ZINC

| 乍 | 空涙 | 2A3 |
| 70G | そらなみだ | * |

Originally crouching dog and door, semantically unclear 戻

| 戻 | レイ、もど-す、もど-る | return, bring back, rebel, bend, vomit | 70G |
| 涙 | ルイ、なみだ | tear | 70G |

| 淚 | VARIANT OF 涙 | tear | 涙 |

INDEX & DEFINITIONS OF ALCHEMICAL SYMBOLS

⌂	1	AIR	Equals breath, breeze, spirit, wind, weather
♏	2	ALEMBIC	Or capitellum (helmet) is a vessel set over the retort to receive and collect vapours
✺	3	ALUM	Grows as hair on fire-resistant salamanders; asbestos
☰	4	AMALGAM	A composition of gold or silver and quick silver
♁	5	ANTIMONY	Also mineral or chemical wolf. Could be used as universal medicine making all other medicine redundant

Symbol	№	Name	Description
♆	6	ARMENIAN BOLE	Red clay, cure against the bite of poisonous snakes
🜨	7	ATHANOR	An oven that is adapted for composing the stone of the philosophers
♏	8	BALM	A preserver of all bodies from destruction and putrefaction
♗	9	BATH OF VAPOURS	A furnace in which the distillatory vase is suspended only over the steam of water in such a manner that the waters do not touch the body
♗	10	BISMUTH	Weissmuth or white substance, bright metal of white colour
⚭	11	BLACK BRIMSTONE	Also horse brimstone, used externally by veterinary surgeons

⊂	12	BLOOD STONE	Synonym for gold
⚭	13	BORAX	Also atincar or rock borax, mineral salt used in foldering, brazing and calling gold
ⅢⅢ	14	BRICK	The plural (Latin lateres) refers to iron tiles
℞	15	CALCINATION	Calcination of bodies is combustion which takes place in a strong heat
ⅩO	16	CAMPHOR	Can be used for medicinal or cullinary purposes
Tm	17	CAPUT MORTUUM	Residue in the retort from which the phlegmatic part has been extracted
☥	18	CINNABAR	Used by Venetian painters because of its blood-colour, also used as an antidote in medicine

♀	19	COPPER, VENUS	A metallic body of bluish colour with a dark ruddy tinge, igneous and fusible
⌦	20	CORAL	A substance that originated from the head of the Medusa
♉	21	CRUCIBLE	A melting vessel made of some earth which can absolutely withstand fire
✧	22	DAY	To be distinguished from Nycthemeron which is night & day: 24 hours
·B	23	DECOCTION	Thick juice made by boiling grain or animal/vegetables
⌣	24	DIGEST	To slowly draw out effective ingredients from drugs by using solvents whilst subjected to stable temperatures

	25	DISSOLUTION	The vaporising of matter and the capture of the condensed moisture thereof in another vessel
	26	DISTILLATION	A process in which the essence is extracted in the form of a liquid
	27	DRAGON'S BLOOD	Synonym for cinnabar, also used as medicine against scratches and the french disease
	28	DRAM	A weight of 3,373 gramm
	29	EARTH	Red earth from lemnos was famous for protecting against poison and plague
	30	EBULLITION	The act, process, or state of boiling or bubbling up

EF	31	EFFERVESCENCE	To escape from a liquid as bubbles; bubble up
℞	32	ELEMENT	The elements are the matrices of substances: fire, air, water, and earth are the four universal matrices
ᴅP	33	EQUAL PARTS	From all parts the same quantity
╬	34	ESSENCE	Essence is a simple extract which contains the whole nature and perfecton of the substances from which it is derived
⇌	35	EXTRACTION	Extraction is the separation of the essential part from the body
⚵	36	FERMENTATION	The incorporation of a fermenting substance with a substance which is to be fermented

Symbol	№	Name	Description
33	37	FILTRATION	Subduction by filtration in a colander; but this process in the chymical filter may also be called straining, or percolation
△	38	FIRE	Fire for the stone of the philosophers
▽	39	FIRST MATTER	Soul and heaven of the elements
♀	40	FIXATION	To make firm, to solidify
♄	41	FLOWERS OF SATURN	Lead oxide, the red form is known as litharge and the yellow form as massicot
⊟	42	FURNACE	A furnace or oven
☿	43	GLASS	Glass, sieve, riddle for distillation, grave, churchyard, because the stone lies hidden therein, and is driven up / down

	44	GLUE OF THE WISE	Special sticky substances used for sealing off the apparatus for distillation
	45	GOLD, SUN	Called sol by the chemists, and dedicated to the sun, is the most tempered of all the metals
	46	GRADE OF FIRE	There are four different grades of fire ranging from tepid to the highest possible level of heat
	47	GRANATE	It is a transparent, ruby-coloured gem, like the blossom of the pomegranate, and is more dusky than the carbuncle

⚭	48	GUM	A transforming substance on account of its adhesive quality. The "glue of the world" (glutinum mundi) is the medium between mind and body
⚲	49	GYPSUM	Its use is chiefly in external application, on account of its extremely drying and destroying nature
⊠	50	HOUR	Time measured by an hourglass
⚔	51	IRON, MARS	This metal is attributed to mars by the chemist, and is so called, because of its many uses in war

♃	52	JUNIPER	Juniper berries are a spice used in a wide variety of culinary dishes and best known for the primary flavouring in gin
♄	53	LEAD, SATURN	Lead with a heavy metallic body, very little whiteness and much of earthy nature
M	54	MAGNESIA	Magnesia is produced when silver and quicksilver are united so as to form a heavy fluid metal. Also the matter of the philospher's stone
X	55	NIGHT	Period of time between sunset and sunrise
♄	56	OIL OF SATURN	Also liquor saturni, lead acetate

Kanji Alchemy II

♛	57	PHILOSOPHICAL STONE	Universal medicine by which age is renewed in youth, metals are transmuted, and all diseases are cured
☿	58	QUICKSILVER, MERCURY	Primary matter of metals, incorporates volatility
℈	59	QUINTESSENCE	A concoction that contains all the powers and qualities of substances in the purest form
	60	RECTIFICATION	Concentration of a fluid through distillation
✕	61	SAL-AMMONIAC	Salmiac, corrosive and desiccating, best from a camel's discharge
☾	62	SILVER, MOON	The luna of chemists, the metal ranked next after gold

♃	63	TIN, JUPITER	Tin, white metallic substance, not pure, livid
⊖⊶	64	VITRIOL	Also roman vitriol, green atrament, a mixture of salt and sulfates
▽	65	WATER	A dry mineral first substance, a catholic water which dissolves all metals
⅀	66	WHITE LEAD	Synonym for tin
⩔	67	WINE	Medicinal drugs used to be mixed with wine
∿	68	YEAR	The annus chymicus or annus philosophicus lasts for 30 days and 30 nights
♌	69	YELLOW AMBER	Once thought to have derived from the seed of wales and worn around the neck as an amulet

亜	70	ZINC	Element: term first used by Paracelsus (1526) due to the form of the crystals after smelting

INDEX SIGNATURE CHARACTERS

亜	ア		next, sub-, Asia	20A
愛	アイ		love	39E
哀	アイ、あわ-れ、あわ-れむ		sorrow, pity	57A
委	イ		committee; entrust to; leave to; devote; discard	26G
医	イ		doctor; medicine	28C
以	イ		start.point, means, use, through, because	38B
胃	イ		stomach	42G
為	イ		do, purpose	56G
尉	イ		military rank	59B
偉	イ、えら-い		great, grand	48C
異	イ、こと		differ, strange	51A
域	イキ		area, limits	51C
員	イン		member, official	25B

隠	イン、かく-す、かく-れる	hide	59D
因	イン、よ-る	cause, be based on, depend on	48A
宇	ウ	eaves, roof, heaven	51D
羽	ウ、は、はね	wing, feather, bird counter	11G
永	エイ、なが-い	long, lasting	30E
易	エキ、イ、やさ-しい	easy, change, divination	43D
園	エン、その	garden, park	6C
鉛	エン、なまり	lead	13F
延	エン、の-びる、の-べる、の-ばす	extend, postpone	53G
炎	エン、ほのお	inflammation, flame, blaze	24D
王	オウ	king	6B
央	オウ	center	32A
桜	オウ、さくら	cherry	9A
乙	オツ	odd, b, 2nd, stylish	61C
卸	おろ-す、おろし	wholesale, grate	60D

音	オン、イン、おと、ね	sound	3G
可	カ	approve, can, should	16E
佳	カ	beautiful, good	42E
渦	カ、うず	whirlpool, eddy	46E
加	カ、くわ-える、くわ-わる	add, join	42F
家	カ、ケ、いえ、や	house, specialist	9D
化	カ、ケ、ば-ける、ば-かす	change, bewitch	2A
果	カ、は-たす、は-てる、は-て	fruit, result, carryout	42B
貝	かい	shellfish	3F
介	カイ	mediate, shell	18C
拐	カイ	deceive, kidnap, bend	40A
戒	カイ、いまし-める	command, admonish	36C
快	カイ、こころよ-い	pleasant, cheerful	24E
壊	カイ、こわ-す、こわ-れる	break, destroy, ruin	60C
灰	カイ、はい	ashes	27C
各	カク、おのおの	each	28D
角	カク、かど、つの	horn, angle	18G

革	カク、かわ	leather, reform	55F
且	か-つ	furthermore, besides	18A
喝	カツ	shout, scold	60B
滑	カツ、すべ-る、なめ-らか	slide, slip, smooth	56E
感	カン	feeling	17C
官	カン	government, official	30D
漢	カン	Han China, man	34F
観	カン	watch, observe	36G
監	カン	supervise, watch	51G
敢	カン	daring, tragic	52C
喚	カン	shout, yell	60E
缶	カン	can, boiler	61F
甘	カン、あま-い、あま-える、-あま-やかす	sweet, presume upon	59G
寒	カン、さむ-い	cold, midwinter	33A
貫	カン、つらぬ-く	pierce	45F
干	カン、ほ-す、ひ-る	dry, defence	23C

巻	カン、ま-く、ま-き	roll, reel, volume	50G
患	カン、わずら-う	disease, afflicted	60A
牙	ガ、ゲ、きば	tusk; fang	41A
我	ガ、われわ、わが	I, self, my	53C
害	ガイ	harm, damage	34A
慨	ガイ	lament, deplore	59A
楽	ガク、ラク、たの-しい、たの-しむ	pleasure, music	12B
眼	ガン、ゲン、まなこ	eye	22D
幾	キ、いく	how many, how much	34C
鬼	キ、おに	devil, demon, ghost	58A
企	キ、くわだ-てる	plan, undertake	63G
貴	キ、たっと-い、とうと-い、たっと-ぶ、とうと-ぶ	precious, revered	51F
机	キ、つくえ	desk, table	54B
基	キ、もと、もとい	base	30A
旧	キュウ	old, past	39F
丘	キュウ、おか	hill	58G

及	キュウ、およ-ぶ、およ-び、およ-ぼす	reach, extend, and	31G
九	キュウ、ク、ここの、ここの-つ	nine	4E
球	キュウ、たま	sphere, ball	23F
弓	キュウ、ゆみ	bow	40F
巨	キョ	huge, giant	61B
居	キョ、い-る	be, reside	43A
虚	キョ、コ	empty, hollow, dip	55C
去	キョ、コ、さ-る	go, leave, past	28A
協	キョウ	cooperate	44C
享	キョウ	receive, have	57C
凶	キョウ	bad luck, disaster	57D
鏡	キョウ、がかみ	mirror	36D
京	キョウ、ケイ	capital	16B
郷	キョウ、ゴウ	village, rural	55E
挟	キョウ、はさ-む、はさ-まる	insert, pinch, squeeze between	61A

橋	キョウ、はし	bridge	24C
斤	キン	ax, weight	15C
禁	キン	ban, forbid	47A
義	ギ	righteousness	37C
疑	ギ、うたが-う	doubt, suspect	56A
暁	ギョウ、あかつき	dawn, light, event	35E
仰	ギョウ、コウ、あお-ぐ、おお-せ	look up, state, respect	61D
玉	ギョク、たま	ball, sphere, coin	1F
吟	ギン	recite	5F
区	ク	ward, section	31F
句	ク	phrase, clause	48F
空	クウ、そら、あ-く、あ-ける、から	sky, empty	4B
屈	クツ	submit, crouch	61E
薫	クン、かお-る	aroma, fragrance, aura	63D
君	クン、きみ	lord, you Mr	32B
具	グ	equip, means	31B

偶	グウ	by chance, spouse, doll	62A
軍	グン	military, army	21C
慶	ケイ	joy	62E
系	ケイ	lineage, connection	6G
径	ケイ	path, direct	26E
渓	ケイ	valley, gorge	63E
敬	ケイ、うやま-う	respect	57F
恵	ケイ、エ、めぐ-む	blessing, kindness	55D
形	ケイ、ギョウ、かた、かたち	shape, pattern	15E
頃	ケイ、ころ	time; about; toward	63A
契	ケイ、ちぎ-る	pledge, join	49B
傑	ケツ	outstanding	62C
穴	ケツ、あな	hole	27A
欠	ケツ、か-ける、か-く	lack	29D
結	ケツ、むす-ぶ、ゆ-う、ゆ-わえる	bind, join, end	40D
県	ケン	prefecture	31A

倹	ケン	thrifty, frugal	41F
顕	ケン	manifest, visible	64D
犬	ケン、いぬ	dog	53D
兼	ケン、か-ねる	combine, unable	60G
堅	ケン、かた-い	firm, solid, hard	62B
拳	ケン、こぶし	fist	49C
建	ケン、コン、た-てる、た-つ	build, erect	33B
見	ケン、み-る、み-える、み-せる	look, see, show	4D
激	ゲキ、はげ-しい	violent, fierce, strong, intense	59E
玄	ゲン	occult, black	50A
元	ゲン、ガン、もと	originally, source	18B
言	ゲン、ゴン、い-う、こと	word, say, speak	19F
原	ゲン、はら	plain, origin	9E
孤	コ	orphan, lonely	61G
顧	コ、かえり-みる	lookback	62G
己	コ、キ、おのれ	I, me, you, self	7E

戸	コ、と	door	9G
古	コ、ふる-い、ふる-す	old	15A
孝	コウ	filia lpiety	13A
洪	コウ	flood, vast	25E
康	コウ	peace, health	34E
航	コウ	sail, voyage	38G
侯	コウ	marquis, lord	41C
講	コウ	lecture	49F
荒	コウ、あら-い、あ-れる、あ-らす	rough, wild, waste	64A
岡	コウ、おか	hill; height; knoll; rising ground	58D
黄	コウ、オウ、き、こ	yellow	9C
考	コウ、かんが-える	consider	19A
甲	コウ、カン	shell, armour, high, 1st, a	57G
行	コウ、ギョウ、アン、い-く、ゆ-く、おこな-う	go, conduct, column	11F
工	コウ、ク	work	7B

幸	コウ、さいわ-い、さち、しあわ-せ	happiness, luck	25D
更	コウ、さら、ふ-ける、ふ-かす	anew, change, again, grow late	32C
高	コウ、たか-い、たか、たか-まる、たか-める	tall, high, sum	16C
耕	コウ、たがや-す	till, plough	48B
広	コウ、ひろ-い、ひろ-まる、ひろ-める、ひろ-がる、ひろ-げる	wide, spacious	8B
交	コウ、まじ-わる、まじ-える、ま-じる、ま-ざる、ま-ぜる、か-う、か-わす	mix, exchange	4F
刻	コク、きざ-む	chop, mince, engrave	50D
黒	コク、くろ、くろ-い	black	13D
谷	コク、たに	valley, gorge	15G
告	コク、つ-げる	proclaim, inform	37E
護	ゴ	defend, protect	50F
誤	ゴ、あやま-る	mistake, mis-	58F
号	ゴウ	number, call, sign	29F
合	ゴウ、ガッ、カッ、あ-う、あ-	meet, join, fit	7F

	わす、あ-わせる		
左	サ、ひだり	left	3B
才	サイ	talent, year of age	11B
債	サイ	debt, loan	44F
栽	サイ	planting	54C
砕	サイ、くだ-く、くだ-ける	break, smash	38C
妻	サイ、つま	wife	14E
采	サイ、と-る	dice; form; appearance; take; colouring; general's baton	39G
最	サイ、もっと-も	most, -est	40C
作	サク、サ、つく-る	make	10B
察	サツ	judge, surmise, realise	29A
皿	さら	dish, bowl, plate	22F
傘	サン、かさ	umbrella, parasol	62D
参	サン、まい-る	attend, go, be in love, be at a loss, 3	40E
山	サン、やま	mountain	1A

座	ザ、すわ-る	seat, sit, gather	54D
司	シ	administer, official	41E
至	シ、いた-る	go, reach, peak	11C
市	シ、いち	city, market	15D
氏	シ、うじ	clan, family, mr	13B
志	シ、こころざ-す、こころざし	will, intent	42D
刺	シ、さ-す、さ-さる	pierce, stab, thorn	58B
支	シ、ささ-える	branch, support	53B
死	シ、し-ぬ	death	21A
子	シ、ス、こ	child	1G
止	シ、と-まる、と-める	stop	11D
旨	シ、むね	tasty, good, gist	22E
紫	シ、むらさき	purple, violet	65D
式	シキ	ceremony, form	23B
識	シキ	knowledge	47F
七	シチ、なな、なな-つ、なの	seven	4A
膝	シツ、ひざ	knee; lap	64B

失	シツ、うしな-う	lose	37F
執	シツ、シュウ、と-る	take, grasp, execute	63B
舎	シャ	house, quarters	47E
車	シャ、くるま	vehicle, chariot	2C
者	シャ、もの	person	23D
尺	シャク	measure, foot	52D
朱	シュ	vermilion, red	54F
首	シュ、くび	head, neck, chief	8E
主	シュ、ス、ぬし、おも	master, owner, main	20B
秋	シュウ、あき	autumn	20D
収	シュウ、おさ-める、おさ-まる	obtain, store, supply	56F
宗	シュウ、ソウ	religion, main	46A
舟	シュウ、ふね、ふな	boat	63C
周	シュウ、まわ-り	circumference, around	12D
叔	シュク	uncle, young brother	65B
宿	シュク、やど、やど-る、やど-す	lodge, shelter, house	32E

出	シュツ、スイ、で-る、だ-す	emerge, put out	23G
俊	シュン	excellence, genius	44G
処	ショ	dealwith, place	56C
庶	ショ	multitude, various, illegitimate	66D
章	ショウ	badge, chapter	26B
尚	ショウ	furthermore, esteem	43F
将	ショウ	command, about to	52E
焦	ショウ、こ-げる、こ-がす、こ-がれる、あせ-る	scorch, fret	67D
象	ショウ、ゾウ	elephant, image	31C
升	ショウ、ます	liquid measure	64G
詔	ショウ、みことのり	imperial edict	33F
宵	ショウ、よい	evening	25G
色	ショク、シキ、いろ	colour, sensuality	7E
娠	シン	pregnancy	28G
辛	シン、から-い	sharp, bitter	14A
心	シン、こころ	heart, feelings	11E

臣	シン、ジン	retainer, subject	43B
進	シン、すす-む、すす-める	advance	22G
真	シン、ま	true, quintessence	22A
身	シン、み	body	20C
申	シン、もう-す	say, expound	10A
字	ジ、あざ	letter, symbol	2F
侍	ジ、さむらい	attend (upon)	10E
自	ジ、シ、みずか-ら	self	17G
事	ジ、ズ、こと	thing, matter, act	15F
耳	ジ、みみ	ear	4C
弱	ジャク、よわ-い、よわ-る、よわ-まる、よわ-める	weak	10C
需	ジュ	need, demand	62F
受	ジュ、う-ける、う-かる	receive	21E
寿	ジュ、ことぶき	longlife, congratulation	65A
充	ジュウ、あ-てる	full, fill, provide	23E
従	ジュウ、ショウ、ジュ、したが	follow, comply	54E

	-う、したが-える		
十	ジュウ、ジッ、とお、と	ten	3C
重	ジュウ、チョウ、え、おも-い、かさ-ねる、かさ-なる	heavy, pile, -fold	25A
述	ジュツ、の-べる	state, relate	41D
盾	ジュン、たて	shield, pretext	65C
縄	ジョウ、なわ	rope, cord	67A
乗	ジョウ、の-る、の-せる	ride, mount, load	21B
譲	ジョウ、ゆず-る	hand over, yield	63F
須	ス、あごひげ、すべか-らく…べ-し	ought; by all means; necessarily	12G
垂	スイ、た-れる、た-らす	suspend, hang down	50E
寸	スン	measure, inch	7D
瀬	せ	shallows, rapids	65F
制	セイ	system, control	47B
斉	セイ	equal, similar	55A
勢	セイ、いきお-い	power, force	35B
西	セイ、サイ、にし	west	14F

青	セイ、ショウ、あお、あお-い	blue, green, young	3E
井	セイ、ショウ、い	well	33G
正	セイ、ショウ、ただ-しい、ただ-す、まさ	correct	5B
星	セイ、ショウ、ほし	star	26F
成	セイ、ジョウ、な-る、な-す	become, make, consist	30C
隻	セキ	one of a pair, ship counter	65G
赤	セキ、シャク、あか、あか-い、あか-らむ、あか-らめる	red	5D
石	セキ、シャク、コク、いし	stone, rock	2E
昔	セキ、シャク、むかし	olden times, past	32D
夕	セキ、ゆう	evening	4G
折	セツ、お-る、おり、お-れる	bend, break, occasion	41B
説	セツ、ゼイ、と-く	preach, explain	16F
宣	セン	promulgate, state	56B
泉	セン、いずみ	spring	17E
先	セン、さき	previous, precede, tip	3A

外	セン、し-める、うらな-う	divine, occupy	12A
銭	セン、ぜに	sen, coin, money	35C
是	ゼ	proper, this	30G
舌	ゼツ、した	tongue	12C
然	ゼン、ネン	duly, thus, so, but	29C
前	ゼン、まえ	before, front	14B
全	ゼン、まった-く	whole, completely	32F
善	ゼン、よ-い	good, virtuous	53F
遡	ソ、さかのぼ-る	goupstream; retrace the past	48G
壮	ソウ	manly, strong, grand, fertile	33E
創	ソウ	start, wound	41G
僧	ソウ	priest	48D
曹	ソウ	official, companion	68D
争	ソウ、あらそ-う	conflict, vie	38A
送	ソウ、おく-る	send	24B
捜	ソウ、さが-す	investigate	66G

相	ソウ、ショウ、あい	mutual, minister, aspect	21G
走	ソウ、はし-る	run	19G
窓	ソウ、まど	window	43G
操	ソウ、みさお、あやつ-る	handle, chastity	55B
即	ソク	immediate, namely, accession	35D
則	ソク	rule, model, standard	39B
足	ソク、あし、た-りる、た-る、た-す	leg, foot, sufficient	3D
息	ソク、いき	breath, rest, child	27E
束	ソク、たば	bundle, manage	31D
尊	ソン、たっと-い、とうと-い、たっと-ぶ、とうと-ぶ	value, esteem, your	53E
蔵	ゾウ、くら	storehouse, harbour	53A
族	ゾク	clan, family	26C
属	ゾク	belong, genus	44D
逮	タイ	chase, seize	66C
帯	タイ、お-びる、おび	wear, zone	33D

替	タイ、か-える、か-わる	exchange, swap	66F
択	タク	choose, select	27B
宅	タク	house, home	52G
卓	タク	table, excel, high	66B
単	タン	simple, single, unit	33C
旦	タン	daybreak; dawn; morning	56D
探	タン、さぐ-る、さが-す	search, probe	26A
台	ダイ、タイ	platform, stand	14C
大	ダイ、タイ、おお、おお-きい、おお-いに	big	1B
代	ダイ、タイ、か-わる、か-える、よ、しろ	replace, world, generation, fee	28F
暖	ダン、あたた-か、あたた-かい、あたた-まる、あたた-める	warm	58C
池	チ、いけ	pond, lake	8G
知	チ、しる	know	17F
築	チク、きず-く	build	46B

中	チュウ、なか	middle, inside, China	1C
虫	チュウ、むし	insect, worm	5G
朝	チョウ、あさ	court, morning	16D
兆	チョウ、きざ-す、きざ-し	sign, omen, trillion	36A
調	チョウ、しら-べる、ととの-う、ととの-える	adjust, investigate, tone, tune	10F
徴	チョウ、しるし	sign, summon, levy	67F
丁	チョウ、テイ	block, exact	2B
鳥	チョウ、とり	bird	46D
長	チョウ、なが-い	long, senior	16A
直	チョク、ジキ、ただ-ちに、なお-す、なお-る	direct, upright, fix	16G
沈	チン、しず-む、しず-める	sink	67G
珍	チン、めずら-しい	rare, curious	64F
追	ツイ、お-う	chase, pursue	28E
通	ツウ、ツ、とお-る、とお-す、かよ-う	pass, way, commute	13E
廷	テイ	court, government office	30B

亭	テイ	pavilion, inn	44B
帝	テイ	emperor	66A
弟	テイ、ダイ、デ、おとうと	younger brother	14D
適	テキ	suitable, fit, go	52B
的	テキ、まと	target, like, adjectival suffix	35G
徹	テツ	go through, clear, remove	68G
田	デン、た	rice field	7A
斗	ト	dipper, measure	9F
刀	トウ、かたな	sword	13C
唐	トウ、から	(T'ang) China	59F
豆	トウ、ズ、まめ	beans, miniature	19D
棟	トウ、むね、むな	ridgepole, building	67B
匿	トク	conceal	54A
屯	トン	barracks, camp, post	47G
豚	トン、ぶた	pig, pork	40G
奴	ド	slave, servant, guy	38E

度	ド、ト、タク、たび	degree, times	22B
土	ド、ト、つち	earth	6A
銅	ドウ	copper	6F
童	ドウ、わらべ	child	24G
那	ナ	what?	45C
内	ナイ、ダイ、うち	inside	8A
南	ナン、ナ、みなみ	south	18E
尼	ニ、あま	nun, priestess	66E
日	ニチ、ジツ、ひ、か	sun, day	1D
乳	ニュウ、ちち、ち	breasts, milk	57E
妊	ニン	pregnant, swollen	45G
忍	ニン、しの-ぶ、しの-ばせる	endure, stealth	50C
能	ノウ	ability, can, Noh	46G
脳	ノウ	brain	54G
派	ハ	faction, send	35F
波	ハ、なみ	wave	27F
博	ハク、バク	extensive, spread,	38D

		gain, gamble	
白	ハク、ビャク、しろ、しら、しろ-い	white	6D
発	ハツ、ホツ	discharge, start, leave	19C
犯	ハン、おか-す	crime, violate, commit, assault	45A
半	ハン、なか-ば	half, middle	19B
反	ハン、ホン、タン、そ-る、そ-らす	oppose, anti, reverse, bend, cloth, measure	21F
煩	ハン、ボン、わずら-う、わずら-わす	trouble, pain, torment	51E
馬	バ、うま、ま	horse	8C
倍	バイ	double, -fold	29B
媒	バイ	intermediary	68E
売	バイ、う-る、う-れる	sell	8F
爆	バク	burst, explode	45D
伐	バツ	attack, cutdown	67C
抜	バツ、ぬ-く、ぬ-ける、ぬ-かす、ぬ-かる	pluck, extract, miss	69G

番	バン	turn, number, guard	15B
非	ヒ	not, un-, fault	27G
卑	ヒ、いや-しい、いや-しむ、いや-しめる	lowly, mean, despise	68F
比	ヒ、くら-べる	compare, ratio	29E
避	ヒ、さ-ける	avoid	69E
必	ヒツ、かなら-ず	necessarily	42C
筆	ヒツ、ふで	writingbrush	12F
票	ヒョウ	vote, label, sign	39D
表	ヒョウ、おもて、あらわ-す、あらわ-れる	show, surface, list	20E
苗	ビョウ、なえ、なわ	seedling, offspring	67E
父	フ、ちち	father	17B
付	フ、つ-ける、つ-く	attach, apply	34D
布	フ、ぬの	cloth, spread	37D
夫	フ、フウ、おっと	husband, man	39A
不	フ、ブ	not, un-, dis-	32G
風	フウ、フ、かぜ、かざ	wind, style	17D

副	フク	deputy, vice-, sub-	24A
復	フク	again, repeat	42A
噴	フン、ふ-く	emit, spout, gush	69F
武	ブ、ム	military, warrior	47C
仏	ブツ、ほとけ	Buddha, France	11A
生	セイ、ショウ、い-きる、い-かす、い-ける、う-まれる、う-む、お-う、は-える、は-やす、き-なま	life, birth, grow	1E
分	ブン、フン、ブ、わ-ける、わ-かれる、わ-かる、わ-かつ	divide, minute, understand	5C
丙	ヘイ	c, 3rd	23A
弊	ヘイ	my (humble), evil, exhaustion	68A
併	ヘイ、あわ-せる	unite, join	70E
並	ヘイ、なみ、なら-べる、なら-ぶ、なら-びに	row, line, rank with, ordinary	49G
兵	ヘイ、ヒョウ	soldier	39C
平	ヘイ、ビョウ、たい-ら、ひら	flat, even, calm	19E
編	ヘン、あ-む	edit, knit, book	51B

変	ヘン、か-わる、か-える	change, strange	37G
片	ヘン、かた	one side, piece	45B
米	ベイ、マイ、こめ	rice, America	20F
補	ホ、おぎな-う	make good, stopgap	57B
保	ホ、たも-つ	preserve, maintain	44E
歩	ホ、ブ、フ、ある-く、あゆ-む	walk	18D
方	ホウ、かた	side, way, square, direction, person	10G
崩	ホウ、くず-れる、くず-す	crumble, collapse	65E
包	ホウ、つつ-む	wrap, envelop	36E
峰	ホウ、みね	peak, top	68C
豊	ホウ、ゆたか	abundant, rich	49E
北	ホク、きた	north, flee	7G
墓	ボ、はか	grave	44A
棒	ボウ	pole, bar, club	58E
冒	ボウ、おか-す	defy, risk, attack	69C
僕	ボク	manservant, I	69A

没	ボツ	sink, disappear, die, lack, not	55G
凡	ボン、ハン	mediocre, common, toughly, in general	68B
麻	マ、あさ	hemp, flax, numb	70F
毎	マイ	each, every	12E
妹	マイ、いもうと	younger sister	5E
末	マツ、バツ、すえ	end, tip	34B
慢	マン	lazy, rude, boastful	69D
妙	ミョウ	exquisite, strange, mystery	14G
民	ミン、たみ	people, populace	35A
矛	ム、ほこ	halberd, lance, spear	46C
明	メイ、ミョウ、あ-かり、あか-るい、あか-るむ、あか-らむ、あき-らか、あ-ける、あ-く、あ-くる、あ-かす	clear, open, bright	7C
面	メン、おも、おもて、つら	face, aspect, mask	27D
免	メン、まぬか-れる	escape, avoid	31E
綿	メン、わた	cotton, cotton wool	48E

茂	モ、しげ-る	grow thickly	59C
盲	モウ	blind	52F
目	モク、ボク、め、ま	eye, ordinal, suffix	2G
門	モン、かど	gate, door	17A
夜	ヤ、よ、よる	night	13G
厄	ヤク	misfortune, disaster	49A
役	ヤク、エキ	role, service, duty	25C
輸	ユ	transport, send	46F
由	ユ、ユウ、ユイ、よし	reason, means, way	30F
悠	ユウ	compose, distant, long time, ample	45E
融	ユウ	dissolve, melt	60F
勇	ユウ、いさ-む	courage; cheer up; bein high spirits; bravery; heroism	43C
憂	ユウ、うれ-える、うれ-い、う-い	grief, sorrow	52A
有	ユウ、ウ、ある	have, exist	29G
雄	ユウ、お、おす	male, powerful	49D

誘	ユウ、さそ-う	invite, tempt, lead	64E
予	ヨ	already, prior, I	18F
与	ヨ、あた-える	give, convey, impart, involvement	21D
余	ヨ、あま-る、あま-す	excess, ample, I	47D
陽	ヨウ	sunny, male, positive (yang)	8D
曜	ヨウ	day of the week	10D
妖	ヨウ、あや-しい、なまめ-く	attractive	43E
要	ヨウ、い-る	need, vital, pivot	34G
羊	ヨウ、ひつじ	sheep	26D
揺	ヨウ、ゆ-れる、ゆ-る、ゆ-らぐ、ゆ-るぐ、ゆ-する、ゆ-さぶる、ゆ-すぶる	shake, swing, rock	69B
利	リ、き-く	profit, gain, effect	36F
里	リ、さと	village, league	9B
陸	リク	land	36B
立	リツ、リュウ、た-つ、た-てる	stand, rise, leave	2D
竜	リュウ、たつ	dragon	64C

留	リュウ、ル、と-める、と-まる	stop, fasten	50B
呂	リョ、ロ	spine; backbone	20G
寮	リョウ	hostel, dormitory	70A
量	リョウ、はか-る	measure, quantity	37A
良	リョウ、よ-い	good	38F
倫	リン	principles, ethics	37B
林	リン、はやし	woods, forest	40B
累	ルイ	accumulate, involve	70B
涙	ルイ、なみだ	tear	70G
令	レイ	order, rule	28B
励	レイ、はげ-む、はげ-ます	encourage, strive	70D
列	レツ	row, line	22C
錬	レン	refine, train, drill	25F
録	ロク	record, inscribe	24F
六	ロク、む、む-つ、むっ-つ、むい	six	5A
腕	ワン、うで	arm, skill	70C

BIBLIOGRAPHY & ONLINE RESOURCES

Coulmas, Florian (1981), Ueber Schrift, Suhrkamp Taschenbuch Wissenschaft
DeFrancis, John (1984), Chinese Language: Fact and Fantasy, University of Hawaii Press
Henshall, Kenneth G. (1995), A Guide to Remembering Japanese Characters, Tuttle
Jim Breen's WWWJDIC [Online] Available http://www.csse.monash.edu.au/ (2014)
Nozaki Kanji Frequency List: [Online] Available http://web.archive.org/web/20080320143000/http://nozaki-lab.ics.aichi-edu.ac.jp/nozaki/asahi/kanji.html (2014)
Ostler, Nicolas (2006), Empires of the Word, Harper Perennial
Rick Harbaugh's Zhongwen Chinese Character Genealogy: [Online] Available http://zhongwen.com/ (2014)
Seeley, Christopher (2000), A History of Writing in Japan, Ateneo de Manilla University Press
Shirakawa, Shizuka (2003), 常用漢字解, Heibonsha
Shirakawa, Shizuka (2006), 人名字解, Heibonsha
Toyoda, Etsuko: 'Enhancing Autonomous L2 Vocabulary Learning Focusing on the Development of Word-Level Processing Skills' 2007 [Online] Available www.readingmatrix.com/articles/etsuko_toyoda/article.pdf (2014)

Alchemy and Astrology

Bobrick, Benson (2006), The Fated Sky: Astrology in History, Simon & Schuster
De Sphaera Mundi [Online] Available 1230
Eliade, Mircea (1979), The Forge and the Crucible: The Origins and Structure of Alchemy, The University of Chicago Press
Gettings, Fred (1981), Dictionary of Occult, Hermetic and Alchemical Sigils, Routledge & Kegan Paul Ltd
Klibansky, Raymond, Panofsky, Erwin, Saxl, Fritz (1992), Saturn und Melancholie: Studien zur Geschichte der Naturphilosophie und

Medizin, der Religion und der Kunst, Suhrkamp Taschenbuch Wissenschaft
Maier, Michael: 'Atalanta Fugiens' 1617 [Online] Available
Poisson, Albert: 'Theories et Symboles des Alchimistes Le Grand Oeuvre' 1891 [Online] Available
http://chrysopee.url.ph/_ouvrages/377.pdf (2014)
Rulandus, Martin: 'A Lexicon of Alchemy or Alchemical Dictionary'1612 [Online] Available
http://www.rexresearch.com/rulandus/rulxa.htm (2014)
Splendor Solis 1532 [Online] Available

Mnemonics

Carruthers, Mary (2008), The Book of Memory: A Study of Memory in Medieval Culture, Cambridge Studies in Medieval Literature
Higbee, Kenneth L. (2001), Your Memory: How It Works and How to Improve It, Da Capo Press
Rossi, Paolo (2000), Logic and the Art of Memory: The Quest for a Universal Language, University of Chicago Press
Yates, Frances (2014), The Art of Memory, Random House UK

www.ingramcontent.com/pod-product-compliance
Lightning Source LLC
Chambersburg PA
CBHW070532010526
44118CB00012B/1108